Pocket Guide to Chicago Architecture

Third Edition

Judith Paine McBrien

Illustrations by John F. DeSalvo

W. W. Norton & Company
New York • London

To Vincent W. Mcbrien

Copyright © 2014, 2004, 1997 by Judith Paine Mcbrien
Copyright © 1993, 1992, 1991 by Perspectives International, Inc.

All rights reserved
Printed in the United States of America

For information about permission to reproduce selections from this book, write to
Permissions, W. W. Norton & Company, Inc., 500 Fifth Avenue, New York, NY 10110

For information about special discounts for bulk
purchases, please contact W. W. Norton Special Sales at
specialsales@wwnorton.com or 800-233-4830

Book design by Karen Dangremond
Composition by Ken Gross
Manufacturing by Edwards Brothers Malloy
Production manager: Leeann Graham

Library of Congress Cataloging-in-Publication Data

Mcbrien, Judith Paine, author.
 Pocket guide to Chicago architecture / Judith Paine Mcbrien ; illustrations by John
F. DeSalvo. — Third Edition.
     pages cm
 Includes index.
 ISBN 978-0-393-73393-8 (pbk.)
1. Architecture—Illinois—Chicago—Guidebooks. 2. Chicago (Ill.)—Buildings,
structures, etc.—Guidebooks. 3. Chicago (Ill.)—Guidebooks. I. DeSalvo, John F.,
illustrator. II. Title.
 NA735.C4M42 2014
 720.9773'11—dc23
                                    2014004861

ISBN: 978-0-393-73393-8 (pbk.)

W. W. Norton & Company, Inc., 500 Fifth Avenue, New York, N.Y. 10110
                        www.wwnorton.com

W. W. Norton & Company Ltd., Castle House, 75/76 Wells Street, London W1T 3QT

0 9 8 7 6 5 4 3 2 1

Contents

Introduction 4

Michigan Avenue 7

The Loop 63

The Riverfront 109

Campus Architecture 155

Glossary 169

Index of Architects 175

Index of Buildings 185

Introduction

From a library conceived as a glass egg to a wavy tower that reimagines the skyscraper form, the new edition of the ever-popular *Pocket Guide to Chicago Architecture* showcases some of the most innovative architecture in Chicago's history.

Who would have thought that a butterfly would serve as the model for a new hospital or that one of the most remarkable new buildings would be built not for condos or corporate clients but for the pleasure of poetry?

Developer Donald Trump makes his Chicago debut with the tall, slinky Trump International Hotel and Tower, located on one of the most prominent sites in the city. Further south, architect Doug Garofalo's Hyde Park Art Center is a study in how to redesign a clunky industrial structure for community creativity. But that's not all, as striking additions to the cityscape reveal how Chicago continues to demand and receive some of the best architecture in the world.

The *Pocket Guide to Chicago Architecture* is divided into four areas: three sections follow popular downtown architecture tour routes— Michigan Avenue, the Loop, and Chicago's Riverfront. A fourth section includes selections from the campuses of Rush University, the Illinois Institute of Technology, and the University of Chicago.

The Michigan Avenue area is a favored location for exciting new buildings. Architect Jeanne Gang, who leads Studio Gang Architects, makes her first appearance in the *Pocket Guide* with Columbia College's clever Chicago Media Production Center as well as the award-winning Aqua Tower. In the midst of the historic Michigan Avenue street wall, Krueck + Sexton created a striking multifaceted glass façade for the Spertus Institute for Jewish Learning and Leadership. Just a block away and connected to Sullivan and Adler's landmark Auditorium Building, a blue and green glass tower designed by VOA signals a new era for

Roosevelt University. Further north, just west of Michigan Avenue on Dearborn and Superior streets is the small, subtle Poetry Foundation headquarters.

Chicago, like all cities, is constantly changing, yet the Loop remains the downtown's commercial core. Within a few short blocks one can see the evolution of the steel-frame skyscraper from some of the earliest built in the world, such as the Reliance Building, to the Willis (formerly Sears) Tower, now the second-tallest building in North America.

The Chicago River, engineered to flow "backward" from Lake Michigan, splits into the north and south branches to form exceptional view corridors for buildings that line its banks through the downtown. Once the home of factories and warehouses, the Riverfront now includes some of the most prestigious corporate and mixed-use structures in the city.

The twenty-first century in Chicago is bringing new attention to universities as developers of some of the most remarkable buildings in this guidebook. The hospital tower at the Rush University Medical Center is a good example. Designed by Ralph Johnson of Perkins + Will, it combines state-of-the-art hospital facilities and sustainable features in an evocative, unusual form. The Illinois Institute of Technology, where Mies van der Rohe once worked, includes a reinterpretation of a campus center by controversial architect Rem Koolhaas while the University of Chicago continues to select leading architects from around the world, such as Billie Tsien and Tod Williams, to implement its expansive campus plan.

Whether you walk through the downtown, take a boat tour along the Chicago River, or visit university neighborhoods, the *Pocket Guide* is a companion to your own discovery of design in a city that understands architecture as a defining element of its character.

Michigan Avenue

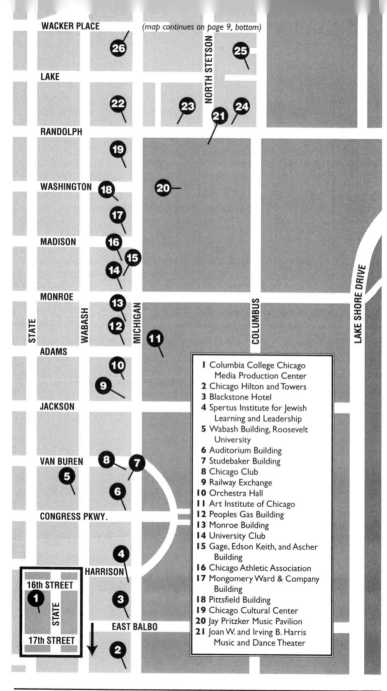

WACKER PLACE

(map continues on page 9, bottom)

NORTH STETSON

26

25

LAKE

22

23

21 **24**

RANDOLPH

19

WASHINGTON **18**

20—

17

16

MADISON

15

14

MONROE

13

12

MICHIGAN

WABASH

STATE

11

COLUMBUS

LAKE SHORE DRIVE

ADAMS

10

9

JACKSON

VAN BUREN **8** **7**

5

6

CONGRESS PKWY.

4

HARRISON

16th STREET

1

STATE

3

EAST BALBO

17th STREET

2

1 Columbia College Chicago
   Media Production Center
2 Chicago Hilton and Towers
3 Blackstone Hotel
4 Spertus Institute for Jewish
   Learning and Leadership
5 Wabash Building, Roosevelt
   University
6 Auditorium Building
7 Studebaker Building
8 Chicago Club
9 Railway Exchange
10 Orchestra Hall
11 Art Institute of Chicago
12 Peoples Gas Building
13 Monroe Building
14 University Club
15 Gage, Edson Keith, and Ascher
   Building
16 Chicago Athletic Association
17 Mongomery Ward & Company
   Building
18 Pittsfield Building
19 Chicago Cultural Center
20 Jay Pritzker Music Pavilion
21 Joan W. and Irving B. Harris
   Music and Dance Theater

OAK

WALTON

DELAWARE

CHESTNUT

PEARSON

CHICAGO

SUPERIOR

HURON

ERIE

ONTARIO

OHIO

GRAND

ILLINOIS

HUBBARD

KINZIE

SOUTH WATER

OHIO

GRAND

SUPERIOR

HURON

LAKE SHORE DRIVE

MIES VAN DER ROHE

DEWITT

FAIRBANKS

FAIRBANKS

McCLURG

STATE

WABASH

RUSH

MICHIGAN

SAINT CLAIR

CHICAGO RIVER

WACKER

22 Associates Center
23 Prudential Plaza
24 Aon Center
25 Aqua Tower
26 Carbide and Carbon Building
27 320 North Michigan Avenue
28 London Guarantee and
   Accident Building
29 333 North Michigan Avenue
30 Michigan Avenue Bridge and
   Bridge Houses
31 Wrigley Building
32 Equitable Building
33 Chicago Tribune Tower
34 Medinah Athletic Club
35 McGraw-Hill Building
36 600 North Fairbanks
37 Lake Shore Trust and
   Savings Bank
38 Woman's Athletic Club
39 Crate & Barrel
40 Allerton House
41 Poetry Foundation
42 Olympia Center
43 Chicago Water Tower and
   Pumping Station
44 Museum of Contemporary Art
45 860/880 Lake Shore Drive
46 Water Tower Place
47 Fourth Presbyterian Church
48 John Hancock Center
49 Sofitel Chicago Water Tower
50 Palmolive Building
51 900 North Michigan Avenue
52 Drake Hotel
53 One Magnificent Mile

(map continues on page 8, top)

Studio Gang Architects
1600 South State Street
2010

For its first new building in 120 years, Columbia College sought a signature structure to coordinate and improve facilities for its best-known programs: film; television; and interactive arts and media. Jeanne Gang's two-story Media Production Center design delivers just that: an eye-catching yet highly functional 35,000-square-foot part-steel frame, part-concrete building that stretches along South State Street not far from the Columbia campus core. Multicolor letters spell "Columbia" on the clear-glass façade that is interspersed with vertical color panels referencing film color bars. Inside, the entry opens to a double-height lobby where six LED media projection screens face open, double-wide gallery seating. An adjacent wall features a remnant of Chicago's heyday as a film center, the salvaged terracotta archway of the Lasky-Famous Player/Paramount Studios. Programmatically, the plan includes three stages and a motion capture studio lined up on the alley side for easy truck and equipment access and a large equipment storage area in the building's center. Facing State Street is the Construction Shop and a ramp that leads upward to two classrooms and the Directing Studio. Both client and architect worked to achieve a LEED Gold certification by using recycled materials, green roofs, and energy-efficient measures.

Holabird and Roche
700–46 South Michigan Avenue
1925–7
Renovation: Solomon Cordwell Buenz and Associates (architects) with
Hirsch/Bedner and Associates (interior designers), 1986
Formerly known as the Stevens Hotel

When this massive, 25-story hotel was completed in the Roaring Twenties, it was the largest in the world, with 3,000 guest rooms, an eighteen-hole rooftop golf course, and its own hospital. The hotel also aspired to be the most elegant, and hence looked to French classical and rococo styles for inspiration. The exterior is grand but subdued. A base and top of Bedford limestone frame the red brick central section, where three large light wells divide the mass into four vertical sections. Inside, however, is all Louis XVI luxe. The Grand Ballroom was modeled after the Palace of Versailles: washed in pinks, cream, and powder blue, it features 24-carat gold leaf and crystal chandeliers and a series of golden arched doorways linked by gilt-framed pastoral murals. The double-story Grand Stair Hall, with marble pilasters and a ceiling of painted clouds, continues the theme. Though the hotel's opening met with rave reviews, hotelier James W. Stevens (1853–1936) was able to enjoy the enterprise only briefly. By 1932, the hotel was in receivership, a victim of the Great Depression; four years later it was bankrupt. Fortunately, a recent renovation has restored its splendid spaces.

Marshall and Fox
630 South Michigan Avenue
1908

The Blackstone was the first high-rise hotel built on Michigan Avenue. Its French Second Empire style represented the ultimate in elegant taste; its creators represented the best of Chicago society. It was developed by John B. (1872–1964) and Tracy C. (1864–1939) Drake, sons of Chicago's noted hotelier John Burroughs Drake; the site was the former home of Timothy Blackstone, a family friend of the Drakes and president of the Chicago and Alton Railroad. When, after the 1871 Chicago Fire, other property types began to replace the fashionable rowhouses that had lined South Michigan Avenue, the pedigreed Blackstone became the hub of Chicago high society activity, accommodating the balls and debutante parties that families had formerly hosted in their homes. Creamy terra cotta is used above the pink granite foundation and again, shaded blue and green-gray, on the upper stories. Twelve stories of dark red brick rise from the base, with windows framed in slightly projecting terra cotta architraves. These are capped by an ornamented mansard roof that once dominated the lakefront skyline. In1910, architects Marshall and Fox designed the five-story granite Blackstone Theater on Balbo Street adjacent to the Blackstone Hotel.

Krueck + Sexton
610 South Michigan Avenue
2007

As groups debated landmark status for the Michigan Boulevard District facing Grant Park and the lakefront, focus turned to a rare vacant lot in the famous street wall: the future site of the Spertus Institute. Could a new building be compatible with its iconic neighbors while satisfying client needs for a dramatic, meaningful presence? The solution, led by architects Ron Krueck (b. 1946) and Mark Sexton (b. 1956) is a ten-story, 145,000-square-foot structure faced with an unusual folded glass surface. This façade adds modernist distinction to the street's historic context, symbolizes the multifaceted mission of the Institute, and maximizes natural light for the deep midblock site. Inside, the building includes classroom facilities for the degree-granting programs, the 400-seat Feinberg Theater for presentations, exhibition space, museum galleries, the Asher Library, a café, and administrative offices. The custom-fabricated triangulated façade consists of 726 lites of insulated glass in 556 unique shapes integrated into an innovative framing system. Y-shaped mullions permit attached brackets to swivel along the horizontal plane while tall vertical mullions were shaped to slope inward or outward beyond the property line. A scissor staircase adds drama to the airy three-story atrium and many sustainable features led to a LEED Silver designation.

VOA Associates
421–425 South Wabash
2012

In 2010, Roosevelt University embarked upon a bold plan: to build a new 414,585-square-foot, 32-story skyscraper campus and connect it to the university's home since 1947, the landmark Auditorium Building completed by Adler and Sullivan in 1889 (see #6). The result is a striking addition to Chicago's skyline that highlights Roosevelt's transition from a part-time commuter school to a full-time residential university experience. Faced with a narrow 100- by 170-foot site on the backside of low-rise historic Michigan Avenue, architect Christopher Groesbeck (b. 1953) designed the building's folding form as a series of stacked rhomboids and clad it in glass panels of varying bluish green and gray to create an ever-changing surface rhythm in sun and shadow. The first six floors are devoted to student activities, and include a second-floor cafeteria and a fitness center; floors 7–13 are state-of-the-art classrooms for science, business, real estate, and executive administration; and floors 14–31 are devoted to residential housing. Mechanicals top the structure. Lucky students: while the dorm rooms are small, the forever-unimpeded views across Grant Park to Lake Michigan are spectacular. Note architect Andrew Rebori's (1886–1966) handsome façade that once graced the Fine Arts Building Annex (1924) and is now incorporated into the new design.

In 1886, Ferdinand Peck, a wealthy young businessman, organized the Chicago Auditorium Association to build a grand cultural and civic center befitting the brash, prosperous city of Chicago. He hired the firm of Adler & Sullivan, a small firm best known for their theater designs, to undertake the monumental multi-use project. They began with a simple, sturdy exterior, featuring a two-story, rough-hewn granite base topped by a floor of rusticated limestone, and above, smooth-faced limestone that created a flat wall plane from the fourth floor to the tower. A 400-room hotel is signaled by three great entrance arches on Michigan Avenue; office space was placed on Wabash Avenue and in the tower. Revenues from these spaces were to fund the heart of the structure: the Auditorium Theater. Here, Louis Sullivan displayed his brilliant designs combining naturalistic and geometric forms. Note how the new electrical illumination becomes an integral part of the composition. Unparalleled acoustics and sight lines were achieved in part by Dankmar Adler's use of a steeply raked auditorium floor and the manipulation of the interior plaster surfaces, including the great arches opening out from the stage. Since 1946, the Auditorium Building has been home to Roosevelt University.

Solon S. Beman
410 South Michigan Avenue
1885; renovation, 1898
Now known as the Fine Arts Building

This eleven-story building was designed by Solon S. Beman (1853–1914) with a Romanesque façade of rough-faced Bedford limestone and granite, and round-arched entries repeated in the upper floors. The Studebaker Building was originally built as a showroom for the Studebaker Carriage Company; carriages were displayed on the first four floors, which have the unusually large windows. Wagons were assembled upstairs. The roofline had a distinct silhouette, with two pyramids and three domes topping the five main bays. When the business moved to larger quarters, Beman was hired to convert the structure to use for artists, writers, and musicians. Two music halls and storefront shops replaced the ground-floor showrooms. The domes, the attic, and the original façade of the eighth floor were removed and replaced with a three-story addition. Renamed the Fine Arts Building in 1898, it contained 65 music studios, offices, and large tenant-artist quarters. Among the tenants were sculptor Lorado Taft; artist William W. Denslow, who drew illustrations for *The Wonderful Wizard of Oz* here; editors of *The Dial* literary magazine; the Municipal Art League; and on the ground floor, Browne's Bookstore, designed by Frank Lloyd Wright, who briefly rented space on the prestigious tenth floor.

Granger and Bollenbacher
81 East Van Buren Street
1930

The twelve-story Chicago Club, constructed of Connecticut brownstone, shares its famous Michigan Avenue block with the Auditorium and Fine Arts buildings. It is an exemplum of contextuality, built long before "contextuality" became a Postmodern mantra, harmonizing with its neighbors in terms of scale, materials, proportion, and detail. Most notable are the block's recurrent two-story rusticated bases, variations in arched windows, and flat roofs. Here, the façade's surface is unornamented; the windows provide an interplay of solid and void that gives the mass a static poise. Burnham and Root's Art Institute (1887) stood on this site and was bought by the Chicago Club in 1893 when the Art Institute moved across the street (see #11). When the older building collapsed during a renovation in 1929, a new building was planned. Note the triple-arched entrance on Van Buren Street, which is a remnant of its distinguished predecessor. The architect, Alfred Hoyt Granger (1867–1939), was active in Chicago civic affairs and was the lone architect on the jury of the famed Chicago Tribune competition in 1922. His Chicago Club, founded in 1869, is among the city's most prestigious enclaves, many of which are located on Michigan Avenue.

D. H. Burnham and Co.
224 South Michigan Avenue
1903–4
Now known by its address

The seventeen-story Railway Exchange, later known as the Santa Fe Building, is one of D. H. Burnham and Co.'s most successful designs. The firm was a major stockholder in the building, and located its offices on the fourteenth floor. Like the firm's earlier Rookery building (1888), the Railway Exchange has a two-story open court, here made square and symmetrical; its mezzanine level is reached by a grand staircase. Above this, the 60- by 70-foot light well is faced in white enameled brick. The exterior walls are faced in a similarly pale cream, enameled terra cotta, and alternate flush and projecting bays in the main section, with flat surfaces at the building's base and top. Bull's-eye windows below the cornice function as both an additional light source and a decorative feature. Other classical motifs include Greek fretwork on the spandrels, antefixae at the cornice, and classical urns at the doorways. Consistent use of white brick and terra cotta recalled the White City of the 1893 Columbian Exposition; it also brightened the environment of Chicago's smoky, railroad-dominated downtown. Enameled terra cotta had a further advantage: city soot could simply be washed off.

D. H. Burnham and Co.
220 South Michigan Avenue
1904
Now known as
Symphony Center

This Neo-Georgian building illustrates the popularity of historic revival-ism at the turn of the century. The corners are marked by quoins, which are topped by decorative swags just below the original cornice. The main four-story section of the building features regularly spaced double-hung windows against a flat brick surface, terminating in a limestone attic. This symmetrical façade highlights three tall, arched windows flanked by pedimented balcony doors on the second floor, behind which is the ballroom. The four-story auditorium is at the rear. The Cliff Dwellers Club was added as a ninth floor in 1908, designed by architect Howard Van Doren Shaw (1869–1926). It is where member Louis Sullivan wrote *The Autobiography of an Idea.* The names of leading composers are incised on the frieze above the second-floor balcony; note also that of Theodore Thomas, below Bach. Thomas was the Chicago Symphony Orchestra's founder and first conductor. Incensed by empty concert seats in the too-large Auditorium Theater (see #6), he demanded the construction of this smaller space on threat of resignation. CSO trustee Daniel Burnham donated his services, and Thomas conducted the first concert here in 1904. Three weeks later he died.

Shepley, Rutan and Coolidge
Michigan Avenue at Adams Street
1892–3

Additions: McClintock Court, Coolidge and Hodgdon, 1924; Ferguson Building, Holabird and Root, 1958; Morton Wing, Shaw, Metz and Associates, 1962; Rubloff Building, Skidmore, Owings & Merrill, 1976; Reconstruction of Stock Exchange Trading Room, Vinci/Kenny, 1977; Rice Building, Hammond, Beeby and Babka, 1988; Modern Wing, Renzo Piano, 2009

Built in conjunction with the World's Columbian Exposition of 1893, which used it for scholarly forums, the limestone Art Institute of Chicago was designed in the Beaux Arts style so prevalent at the Fair. Its symmetrical massing and classical decorative elements create a dignified exterior. The first-story walls are of rusticated limestone; the second, taller story has a smooth ashlar finish punctuated by a series of sculpture arcades and capped by a frieze reproducing the Parthenon's Panathenaic procession. Note the artists' names inscribed on the architrave. Interior spaces are organized in corridors off a grand central staircase. Established in 1879 as the Academy of Fine Arts, the museum grew quickly; by 1893, it had replaced W. W. Boyington's 1873 Inter-State Exposition Building in Lakefront (now Grant) Park. Sculptor Edward Kemeys (1843–1907) is responsible for the famous lions, symbols of strength and majesty, which have flanked the entrance since 1894. Over the past century, many additions have been constructed; the museum and its School now straddle the railroad tracks that once bounded the museum's east façade. Gardens on the south, designed by landscape architect Dan Kiley, and on the north by Hanna/Olin, are important components of the museum's design tradition.

D. H. Burnham and Co.
122 South Michigan Avenue
1911

The 22-story Peoples Gas Building stands on the site of Burnham and Root's Brunswick Hotel (1883), which in turn replaced the elegant H. H. Honore family home, where Bertha Honore married Potter Palmer. Huge granite columns march across the base of the building, but the weight of the exterior walls is actually carried on cantilevered girders at the second floor line. Like the nearby Railway Exchange building (see #9), also by D. H. Burnham and Co., a central light court opens above the third floor. The façade is divided into three parts: a columnar base, a textured shaft with pairs of regularly spaced double-hung windows, and from the seventeenth to twentieth floors, a colonnade made to look like granite, which is terra cotta instead. The corners are marked by flat piers, also of terra cotta. Originally, customer service was located in the central light court, in a room surrounded by two tiers of marble columns and topped by a Tiffany glass ceiling. Corporate pride extended to the building's private spaces, where state-of-the-art amenities included lavatories for every office suite, pneumatic cleaning equipment, and a public stenographer's office.

Holabird and Roche
104 South Michigan Avenue
1912

Designed in the Italian Gothic style, the sixteen-story Monroe Building was built to harmonize with the newly completed University Club on the opposite corner, also by Holabird and Roche (see #14). For example, its flat roof was changed to a gabled peak to repeat the University Club's silhouette, and its ornamental language is similarly historic. Above the twelfth story, the gable is emphasized by bifora windows that are smaller at the sides, and culminate in a double-storied window at the peak. Its first two stories are of pink-gray granite; the color scheme is continued above in matching terra cotta. The interior is equally remarkable: hallway and vestibules are of Rookwood tile, which is also used for the floors and wainscoting of the upper corridors of the building. Rookwood tile was popular during the Arts and Crafts movement in America and is characterized by the use of pastels and subtle glazing. Now home to the Pritzker Military Museum, the property was developed by Shepherd Brooks of Boston, who, with his brother Peter (1831–1920), developed many of Chicago's best-known buildings after the 1871 Chicago Fire, including the Monadnock, Marquette, and Pontiac buildings.

Holabird and Roche
26 East Monroe
1908–9

The University Club was formed in 1887 by a group of college graduates whose purpose was "the promotion of literature and art, by establishing and maintaining a library, reading room, and gallery of art." After twenty years of meeting in various quarters downtown, the association planned a building of its own. The twelve-story University Club rises at the corner of Monroe Street and Michigan Avenue on a steel skeletal frame, the same structural system used a decade earlier by the same architects for the neighboring Gage Group (see #15). But while those buildings express their internal cage, the University Club dresses its frame in Gothic robes and ornamentation, a style considered appropriate to its academic ties. This dignified, symmetrical façade cloaks a variety of functions: athletic facilities, meeting rooms, restaurants, a library, and rooms for overnight accommodations. On the second floor, the Michigan Room combines paneling and wood carving by architect Martin Roche with 56 ceiling panel paintings by club member Frederic Clay Bartlett (1873–1953), a noted art collector who donated Seurat's *Sunday Afternoon on the Island of Grand Jatte* to the Art Institute. Bartlett also designed the fourteen stained-glass windows in the three-story Cathedral Hall on the ninth floor.

Holabird and Roche
18, 24–28, and 30 South Michigan Avenue
1898–9
Now known as the Gage Group

In 1899, the Ascher, Edson Keith, and Gage companies, millinery wholesalers, relocated from quarters on Wabash Avenue to this new complex,
which allowed each firm its own building and the greater natural light
offered by lakefront exposure. These buildings, now known collectively
as the Gage Group, have undergone several alterations and additions,
but they remain a striking example of how an underlying steel structure
can be expressed simply and directly on the exterior. The Ascher and
Keith façades consist of unornamented brick and terra cotta horizontal
spandrels and vertical piers, creating a series of spaces filled by large,
light-maximizing Chicago style windows, in which the fixed pane is flanked
by a movable sash at each side. The taller Gage Building has an identical
frame, but distinguishes itself with a façade designed by Louis Sullivan
(1856–1924). The cream terra cotta tile is decorated by two exuberant
foliate forms exploding atop the piers and by smaller decorative forms
repeated on the spandrels. The windows are composed of four casements
below a band of Luxfer glass; the prismatic qualities of Luxfer glass created
greater light diffusion, a recurrent concern in these designs and elsewhere
before the widespread use of artificial light.

Henry Ives Cobb
12 South Michigan Avenue
1893

This eleven-story Venetian fantasy adds variety and interest to the wall of the buildings along Michigan Avenue. When completed, it boasted of having the largest number of athletic facilities under one roof. The top two floors contain a great dining hall. Architect Henry Ives Cobb (1859–1931) was comfortable working in a variety of architectural styles, including Richardson Romanesque for the Newberry Library and former Chicago Historical Society, both 1892, as well as English Gothic for the first buildings of the University of Chicago. Among his best known designs was Potter Palmer's "castle" mansion on Lake Shore Drive (1882), which he designed in partnership with Charles Sumner Frost. In this clubhouse, he uses narrow lancet windows and tracery as decorative devices, and animates the façade with delicate brickwork. Note the frieze just below the cornice line; it features whimsical paired racquets in relief. Club architecture offered creative possibilities for design, as can be seen in other buildings on Michigan Avenue, such as the former Medinah Athletic Club (see #34), the University Club (see #14), and the Woman's Athletic Club (see #38).

Richard E. Schmidt
6 North Michigan Avenue
1897–9
Addition: Holabird and Roche
c. 1923

Once the headquarters for the Montgomery Ward & Company, founded in 1872, this brick and terra cotta building was for many years the dominant tower on South Michigan Avenue. Located at the corner of Madison Street, it also marks the southern edge of Chicago's original grid: North Michigan Avenue officially begins here. Ward's mail-order business rapidly expanded along the block from its first location on the corner of Michigan Avenue and Washington Street, and finally a large new headquarters was commissioned. Containing warehouse distribution, marketing, and administrative functions under one roof, the building was nicknamed the "Busy Bee-Hive." Above a twelve-story base, a distinctive ten-story tower was topped by a famous gilded, electrically lit nude weathervane, *Progress Lighting the Way for Commerce*. The Montgomery Ward Building established the reputation of Richard E. Schmidt (1865–1958), who worked in association with Hugh M. G. Garden (1873–1961), later his partner. Numerous alterations to this building, including the demolition of the top five stories of the tower, have left it sadly disfigured. In 1908, the company relocated, for better transportation access and more space, to a new facility along the Chicago River designed by Schmidt, Garden, and Martin.

With its copper-roofed tower, the highest in the city when completed, the 38-story Pittsfield Building is a striking landmark just west of Michigan Avenue. It was developed by the Field estate in 1926. In 1922, the City of Chicago raised the height restriction on buildings to 264 feet, provided that the tower did not exceed one-quarter of the building's footprint or one-sixth its volume. Setbacks of one foot in ten from all sides of the adjacent property were also required. This 557-foot-tall skyscraper fulfilled these requirements with setbacks at the twenty-second, thirty-fifth, and thirty-eighth floors, which were emphasized with Gothic turrets. The polished black granite base, however, anticipates the Art Deco style, marking this building as a transitional one. The marriage of this most distinguished Chicago architectural firm and most prominent Chicago family would foster a continued evolution toward the modern aesthetic, in which massing dominates surface detail, as seen in the Field Building at 135 South LaSalle Street (1934). Although the offices in the Pittsfield Building were planned for medical tenants and related professionals, the building's five-story interior atrium uses rich marbles and brass details to create an elegant retail statement. Don't miss the elevator cabs and lobby mailbox.

Shepley, Rutan and Coolidge
78 East Washington Street
1897
Formerly the Chicago Public Library

A restrained Italian Renaissance design, this four-story building of Bedford limestone and granite was the first permanent home of the Chicago Public Library, which began in 1871 as a depository for books donated by Great Britain after the Great Fire. It was built on the site of Dearborn Park and relates to the nearby Art Institute (see #11), also by Shepley, Rutan and Coolidge, in its low-scale, symmetrical form, use of repeating arches, and classical ornamental language. The interior includes remarkable mosaics from the House of Tiffany, executed by J. A. Holzer, including rotundas at the north and south with domes of Tiffany glass. The principal entrance is on Washington Street, where a grand staircase of white Carrara marble leads upward along mosaic-inlaid balustrades. On the Randolph Street side, a staircase leads to the Grand Army of the Republic Memorial Hall on the second floor. The Library Board included this hall in order to utilize the entire Dearborn Park site, part of which had been previously granted to a Civil War veterans group by the Illinois legislature. After Chicago's new library was completed in 1991, this building became Chicago's Cultural Center, which sponsors events and exhibitions for the community.

Billowing curved stainless steel sections surround the open-air stage of Frank Gehry's (b. 1921) music pavilion, the architect's first foray into Chicago. This shiny complex has three main components. The first is the sculptural stage that highlights the orchestra and includes an additional terrace for up to 150 choral members. Glass doors close off the stage so that it can be heated or air-conditioned for smaller performances or events. The second component is a giant horizontal trellis that hovers up to 60 feet above the lawn and covers an oval-shaped area that is 320 by 700 feet. Made of steel piping and columns, the purpose of the trellis is to distribute sound over the Great Lawn, which seats 4,000 people and can accommodate 7,000 more. Developed by Gehry's team, the Great Lawn trellis is equipped with speakers every 65 feet, offers accent lighting capability, and represents the first permanent installation of its kind in the United States. The third component of this complex is a swirling, silver-colored bridge that snakes across Columbus Drive and serves as an access and connection point between the bandshell and the lakefront.

Hammond Beeby Rupert Ainge Architects
205 East Randolph Street
2002–3

This project presented many challenges. First, the building had to be almost entirely underground in order to fulfill Grant Park's proviso that no new permanent buildings be built in the park—it must remain "forever open, clear, and free." The entrance pavilion, serving as both sign and symbol, is 40 feet tall, enclosed in glass, and filled with Louise Nevelson's artwork. Next, the architect was required, on a limited budget, to meet the performance needs of a dozen music, dance, and arts groups who share the facility. The spaces had to be both intimate and grand, and offer good sightlines and acoustics. The solution was to use pre-cast concrete to frame the theater, steeply pitch the rows of seats, add a balcony to accommodate overflow, and include space for an orchestra pit. In addition, triangular steel towers frame the stage and contain acoustical wood panels that act as state-of-the-art sound reflectors. Artificial lighting is a key element, both in the audience chamber where patterned theater lights play, as well as in the public spaces where color-coded fluorescent lighting indicates floors and functions. To the architectural team led by noted designer and educator Thomas Beeby (b. 1941), take a bow!

Overwhelming from street level, this speculative office building rends the fabric of Michigan Avenue by violating that which makes the buildings of the boulevard extraordinary—scale, siting, materials, proportion, and pedestrian amenities. The fourteen-story, masonry-clad John Crerar Library (1920) by Holabird and Roche was demolished for this structure. Its 41-story height dwarfs the Beaux Arts Cultural Center to the south; more important, it lacks the one- or two-story bases that connect the disparate buildings of this boulevard and relate them, regardless of size, to human scale. Instead of stone, brick, or terra cotta, its façade is horizontal aluminum banding, which has the effect of pulling the building out at the sides instead of soaring tall. It is placed on a 45-degree angle to the street, breaking the wall formed by the flush orientation of buildings on the edge of the grid facing the lakefront. Addressing Grant Park on a diagonal, its roofline sliced into two triangular towers, it stands thick and insistent on one of Chicago's most visible corners. It is best seen at night, when white lights outline the diamond-shaped roofline against the darkness.

138 East Randolph Street
Naess and Murphy
1952–5
Addition: C.F. Murphy
and Associates, 1968
180 North Stetson Avenue
Loebl Schlossman and Hackl
1990

This complex is located on a 3.3-acre site over the Illinois Central rail-yards, which stretch across 80 acres from Randolph Street north to the Chicago River and east to Lake Michigan. The 41-story One Prudential Plaza was the first skyscraper built after World War II in Chicago, replacing Holabird and Root's Board of Trade (1930) (see Loop, #8) as the tallest building in the city. When completed in 1955, its flat-topped Indiana limestone slab with the company's name in red neon letters became a highly visible addition to the city's skyline. On the south façade between the eighth and eleventh floors, note the Rock of Gibraltar sculptural relief by Alfonso Ianelli (1889–1965), best known for his work on Frank Lloyd Wright's Midway Gardens. Thirty-five years later, Two Prudential Plaza was completed, designed by Loebl, Schlossman and Hackl, architects of Water Tower Place (see #46). Built of gray granite, to harmonize with the earlier building, and silver glass, this 64-story skyscraper is a sleek tower culminating in a multi-faceted peak and spire, reminiscent of New York's Chrysler Building. The two buildings share a common lobby level and are connected by two five-story atria.

Edward Durell Stone and Perkins and Will Partnership
200 East Randolph Street
1973
Formerly the Standard Oil Building

The stone-clad Aon Center is all about height. Its form, if short, would bore: just another freestanding, flat-topped, square-based mass that is striped with vertical recessed windows. Instead as the 83-story structure rose upward 1,136 feet in 1973 it became not only a towering presence on Chicago's lakefront but also the fifth-tallest building in the world. Edward Durell Stone (1902–1978) was among the country's best-known architects when the Standard Oil Company of Indiana hired him to design its new headquarters on part of the former Illinois Central rail yards. An early modernist, Stone received many prestigious commissions, including the General Motors Building in Manhattan, the Albany campus of the State University of New York, and the United States Embassy in New Delhi, India. However, his Chicago work, done late in his career, disappoints. Even the Carrera marble that Stone insisted upon to sheath his skyscraper began to buckle from Midwest temperature differentials. By 1989, citing safety concerns, the corporation decided to replace the entire marble façade with thicker granite panels at a whopping cost of more than $60 million dollars. Still, like Manhattan's twin towers before they became fabled, the building has earned respect. It may not inspire but it doesn't offend.

Studio Gang Architects
225 North Columbus Drive
2010

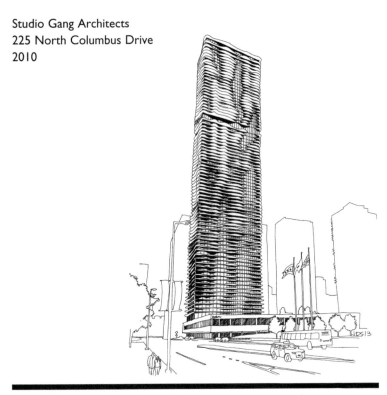

Aqua Tower, an 82-story, 1,900,000-square-foot mixed-use tower on Chicago's lakefront, drew attention long before completion. Women rarely receive skyscraper commissions: it would be a first for Jeanne Gang (b. 1964) and her office. However, what sustained interest was the building's imaginative form. Curving concrete balconies grace the full height of the freestanding building. These cantilevered terraces vary by size and shape on every floor depending on view corridors, sunshade, and the size of the dwelling units. Some units have no balcony and appear as a void on the façade while other units have balconies that extend a few inches to 12 feet. It's as if the building is wrapped with topographic contour map lines. There is nothing new about cantilevered balconies: Gang's bold concept was to understand that today's mobile technology makes it possible to construct unique concrete formwork silhouettes on-site for each floor slab during the concrete pour. The result is a surface ruffling or rippling effect suggestive of wind or waves. The irregular surface helps disperse powerful wind forces while being highly photogenic. Although some fear that the thermal differential between inside and outside could cause cracks in the concrete balconies, Aqua has been widely praised for its originality.

Burnham Brothers
230 North Michigan Avenue
1929

This 40-story skyscraper is characterized by a series of setbacks that reflect the 1922 zoning ordinance aimed at providing more light at street level. What distinguishes the Carbide and Carbon Building among the monochromatic high-rises of Chicago is its coloring: polished black granite at the base, with shades of dark-green mottled terra cotta on floors four through twenty-six. Gold terra cotta accents the piers and pilasters at the top of the building, and marks the flower medallions at the top of the black granite base. Note too the swirling grillwork at the entrance. This decorative language is carried into the lobby, which has a gray Tennessee marble floor with a Belgian black marble border and bronze metalwork above the entrance, on elevators, and fixtures. Daniel (1886–1961) and Hubert (1882–1969) Burnham were sons of noted Chicago architect and planner Daniel Hudson Burnham; they designed several commercial buildings and hotels in the city, including the Bankers Building and the Seneca Hotel, both 1927. The building's form was inspired by the shape of a champagne bottle, so the story goes. True or not, its sparkling top and telescoping mass provide an exuberant reminder of Chicago in the boisterous, carefree Twenties.

Booth/Hansen & Associates
1983

Built on a narrow 48-foot-wide lot, this 26-story structure, now a hotel, was built as a mixed-use project including two levels of below-grade parking, retail space on the ground floor, offices on floors two through thirteen and residential condominiums above. Its continuous piers separate the exterior into three bays and carry the eye upward, culminating in splayed capitals intersected by a glass gabled penthouse. Setbacks on the top three stories allow for terraces that add interest to the façade and create spectacular views for the guests. Architect Laurence Booth (b. 1936) used wide Chicago windows to create a regular rhythm on the façade. At the base, he fashioned double-story columns with an ogee curve that hides imperfections and water stains in the poured concrete, an imaginative solution to a budgetary constraint. Blank side walls of pink stucco assume future adjacent construction, but meanwhile, windows have been punched in for additional light and views. Trained at Harvard and the Massachusetts Institute of Technology and winner of numerous local and national design awards, Booth has designed apartments, residences, and adaptive reuse projects. Here he has created a slender, understated structure that adds dignity to the historic boulevard.

Alfred S. Alschuler
360 North Michigan Avenue
1922–3

As the Wrigley Building (see #31) was nearing completion, Alfred Alschuler (1876–1940) received a plum commission: the headquarters building for the London Guarantee & Accident Company, which would occupy the prominent site just across the Chicago River at the termination of Wacker Drive with the new Michigan Avenue Bridge. Alschuler was known primarily for his industrial work, although he also designed the terra cotta Thompson Building (1912) at 350 North Clark Street, the K. A. M. Isaiah-Israel Synagogue in Chicago's Kenwood neighborhood, and the old Chicago Mercantile Exchange (1927) at 110 North Franklin Street. Here, on the historic site of Fort Dearborn, he designed a 22-story Indiana limestone building using classical references throughout, from the three-story columns marking the entrance, repeated above the fifteenth floor, to the Greco-Roman tempietto on top. This aesthetic is consistent with Burnham's 1909 Plan of Chicago, which envisioned the development of the riverfront in the grand Beaux Arts tradition. Note how the rusticated base matches that of the Wacker Drive Esplanade below and how the unusual concave façade accommodates the semicircular plaza defining the intersection of Michigan Avenue with Wacker Drive.

Holabird and Root
1927–8

The last-built of the four original buildings located at the Michigan Avenue Bridge, 333 North Michigan Avenue resembles a slender gatepost when seen from the length of North Michigan Avenue. Clad in granite and limestone, its design reflects the sleek, Art Deco aesthetic of its time: the mass of the eleven-story tower rising from the 24-story main block is modified by a series of setbacks that emphasize its verticality, as does the absence of a cornice. At the fifth floor of the building are a series of seven-foot-high bas-reliefs by sculptor Fred M. Torrey depicting the growth and early history of Chicago: The Portage, the Hunter, Pioneer Women, the Attack on Fort Dearborn, the Covered Wagon Era, and the Traders. These reliefs harmonize with the overall massing of the building in their bold, simplified lines; they also typify the interest of the era in incorporating sculptural design into the architectural program. Holabird and Root, formed in 1928, was the successor firm to Holabird and Roche and continues to practice today. Its notable designs include the Palmolive Building (see #50), the Chicago Daily News Building (1925–9) (see Riverfront, #21), and the Chicago Board of Trade (1929–30) (see Loop, #8).

Edward H. Bennett, architect; Thomas Pihlfeldt, engineer of bridges; Hugh Young, engineer of bridge design; Henry Herring and J. E. Fraser, sculptors

Michigan Avenue and the Chicago River

1918–20; Pylon sculptures, 1928

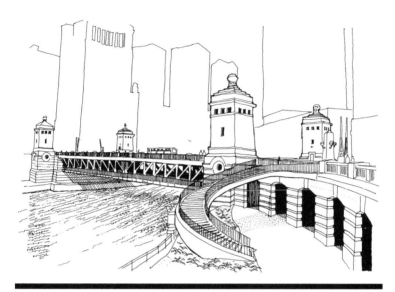

The Michigan Avenue Bridge blended the Beaux Arts aesthetics of Daniel Burnham's 1909 Plan of Chicago with the sophisticated engineering necessary to solve one of Chicago's worst transportation problems. Before 1920, when Michigan Avenue still ended at the river, nearly half of Chicago's north-south traffic converged at the old Rush Street swing bridge, which was also among the first bridges encountered by ships entering from the lake. To ease the resulting congestion, Chicago engineers perfected a bridge type in which leaves divide, rotate around a trunnion pin, and return to their fixed positions. The Michigan Avenue Bridge was their masterpiece: the world's first double-leaf, double-deck trunnion bascule bridge, capable of handling two levels of traffic and still clearing the channel in under 60 seconds. Much of Burnham's grand, classical design, modeled after the Seine bridges of Paris, was implemented after Burnham's death by Edward Bennett (1874–1954), consultant to the Chicago Plan Commission. Bennett's four limestone bridge houses create a monumental approach to this important crossing, while commemorative sculptures by J. E. Fraser and Henry Herring mark the historic location, spanning the sites of Fort Dearborn and Chicago's first pioneer homesteads.

Graham, Anderson, Probst and White
410 North Michigan Avenue
1919–22 (south tower); 1924–5 (north tower)

The Wrigley Building may be Chicago's favorite landmark. Its gleaming white façade and gently curving entrance plaza convey a bright, welcoming feeling; most familiar of all is the eleven-story clocktower, inspired by the Giralda Tower in Seville, Spain, which has also been spotlit at night from the outset. The building was developed by William Wrigley, founder of the chewing gum company, and was, for many years, the Wrigley Company headquarters. As the first building completed north of the Chicago River on the newly extended Michigan Avenue, it initiated the area's redevelopment from a dingy warehouse district to a desirable commercial address. A second building was added to the north in 1925, and is connected to the first at the lobby and by an upper-level skywalk. Both are sheathed in terra cotta, a material popular both for its decorative potential, and for its fireproofing ability, not underestimated in a city leveled by fire just 50 years before. To encourage public access to the Chicago River, a monumental staircase was designed that leads from the entrance plaza to a riverside landing where tour boats dock in the summertime.

On this site, pioneer Jean Baptiste du Sable, Chicago's first permanent settler, built his cabin. Now a 35-story office tower of glazed bronze solar glass with an aluminum curtain wall rises, recalling the structurally expressive style of noted architect Ludwig Mies van der Rohe (1886–1969). This aesthetic was often used by Skidmore, Owings & Merrill in its commercial high-rise designs. Here design partner Bruce Graham (1925–2010) used granite spandrels to mark the floors, while slender vertical piers containing circular pipes divide the windows into sets of four. This pattern gives the façade a subtle rhythm, enhanced when the Chicago River is reflected in the glass. The Chicago Tribune sold the land to the Equitable Life Assurance Society on condition that the new structure be no taller than the Tribune Tower and that, set back from Michigan Avenue, it not obstruct the Tribune's views. Pioneer Court, a plaza connecting the two buildings, is often used for summertime art exhibitions; via a sweeping spiral staircase, it also provides public access to the riverbank below. Such access was an amenity envisioned in the 1909 Plan of Chicago by architects Daniel Burnham and Edward Bennett.

Tower, Hood and Howells; printing plant, Jarvis Hunt
435 North Michigan Avenue
Tower, 1922–5; printing plant, 1916–20

In 1922, the Chicago Tribune announced what became one of the twentieth century's most famous architectural competitions: $100,000 in prize money to design its new headquarters on a site near the just-completed Michigan Avenue Bridge and adjacent to the Tribune's new printing plant on the Chicago River, where the waterway facilitated shipment of newsprint and other operations. The 264 competition entries from around the world included a fascinating range of designs for "the world's most beautiful office building." The winning entry, by Raymond Hood and John Mead Howells of New York, dresses a plain limestone shaft with the gargoyle gutters and flamboyant flying buttresses of France's great Gothic cathedrals. The grand arched entry and surrounding allegorical figures are impressive, but the tower steals the scene: a crown of open tracery that remains as visible and photogenic today as it was in 1922. Ironically, the contest's most influential entry may not have been the winner, but Finnish architect Eliel Saarinen's second-place design. Its strongly rooted and elegantly set-back mass helped define the skyscraper form for the rest of the century. Hood himself referred to it in his later designs in New York for the Daily News Building and Rockefeller Center complex.

Walter W. Alschlager
505 North Michigan Avenue
1929
Now known as the Inter-Continental Hotel

Originally the private, men-only Medinah Athletic Club, this 45-story limestone building was commissioned at the height of the 1920s by the Medinah Nobles, an affiliate of the Shriners with purported roots in the Middle East. Its exotic, eclectic design reflects these presumed origins: note the gold onion dome at the top, and the Assyrian and Egyptian figures carved by Leon Harmart (1866–1936) that grace the façade. These relief sculptures celebrate the builder's trade and the legendary origin of the Freemasons (or stonemasons) guild in England, a forerunner of the Shriners' philanthropic organization, which is known today for its circus and hospitals. Inside, public rooms range in style from an English Tudor Hall to a Spanish Tea Court to a grand Stair Hall of Lions. Athletic facilities, unmatched at the time of completion, included a rifle range and miniature golf courses. A thorough renovation, sensitive to the building's stylistic eccentricity, was completed by Harry Weese and Associates. Today, the Hotel Inter-Continental is an exuberant, idiosyncratic complement to neighboring 1920s designs, the famous Tribune Tower (see #33) next door and the Wrigley Building (see #31) across the avenue.

Thielbar and Fugard
520 North Michigan Avenue
1927–9

Designed by Chicago architects Frederick J. Thielbar and John Reed Fugard, the McGraw-Hill Building is a collaboration between one of the city's leading architectural firms and the sculptors Eugene and Gwen Lux. Gwen Lux (1908–86) is among America's pioneer women sculptors; her work can be found at the Rockefeller Center complex in New York City and at the General Motors Technical Center, designed by architect Eero Saarinen, in Detroit. Note the series of limestone panels depicting figures of Greek mythology and the zodiac. The McGraw-Hill Building served as the midwestern headquarters for the McGraw-Hill publishing company. This elegant limestone Art Deco tower also exemplifies the development of Michigan Avenue north of the Chicago River in the 1920s after the opening of the Michigan Avenue Bridge. The North Central Association worked closely with architects and developers to ensure the highest quality design and uses for this prestigious boulevard. In an historic preservation compromise, this building was dismantled, a new interior shopping mall developed, and the building exterior reconstructed to match the original.

JAHN
600 North Fairbanks Court
2008

The ever-inventive Helmut Jahn has a name for his creative approach: he calls it Archi-Neering. The term refers to his interest in combining mini-malist design with engineering sophistication. His frequent collaborator is German engineer Werner Sobek (b. 1953). Two recently completed examples are the Mansueto Library (see Campus Architecture #5) and 600 North Fairbanks, Jahn's first high-rise residential project in North America. This 41-story glass tower is both spacious and spare. For instance, the lobby boasts a generous 20-foot-high ceiling but the walls and columns are exposed concrete. Note how the building's footprint is outlined as a glass rim lifted above the roof deck. Many skyscrapers accentuate their height with antennas, peaks or towers. Not so here. Jahn crowns his building with something less expected: a void. The façade is clad in large 10- by 7-foot glass panels with no mullions to increase trans-parency. They have a mesh screen on the lower floors masking parking and mechanicals but are clear for the 212 residential units above. Four vertical tiers of indented balconies draw the eye upward and animate the north and south façades, On the west side, the developers secured air rights from the adjacent low-rise property, allowing cantilevered floors to be built that maximize the tower's square footage.

Marshall and Fox
605 North Michigan Avenue
1921–2
Now known as JPMorgan Chase

Benjamin Marshall (1874–1940) and Charles Fox (1870–1926) founded their firm in 1905 and enjoyed great success in Chicago, especially after World War I. Their clientele included well-heeled families and establishments: they designed the Drake Hotel (see #46) on North Michigan Avenue and the lakefront, and today Marshall's luxury apartment buildings on nearby East Lake Shore Drive form the nucleus of the East Lake Shore Drive Historic District. The Lake Shore Trust and Savings Bank has a five-story limestone façade with full-height Corinthian columns flanked by rectangular piers that anchor the building. Many banks are classically styled, but here the cubic envelope creates a simple volume that is stripped of extraneous elements, such as pediments, sculptural reliefs, or figures. The Lake Shore Trust and Savings Bank was organized by prominent members of the North Central Business District Association, many of whom were real estate developers. In this bank, they found a forthright expression to symbolize their financial faith in the new North Michigan Avenue and in Chicago's future.

Familiar with a range of historical styles and skilled at using them effectively, architect Philip Brooks Maher adapted French Second Empire forms for this building, contributing to the Parisian-influenced development of North Michigan Avenue in the 1920s. Maher (1894–1981), the son of Prairie School architect George W. Maher, designed more buildings on North Michigan Avenue than anyone but the large firm Holabird and Root. Many of these structures have been demolished, but the Farwell building at 664 North Michigan Avenue, now a parking garage, and this building remain. In this nine-story structure, home to the country's oldest women's athletic facility, a number of nonathletic functions were accommodated. The first floor was devoted to swank retail shops; the second, or *piano nobile*, was reserved for public occasions; the crowning seventh and eighth floors were designed for a grand ballroom in which large social gatherings were held. The window treatments mark these special uses: a Palladian window heralds the second floor on Ontario Street, while on the upper stories niches housing winged griffins flank large windows decorated with swags and bucrania (ox skulls with garland-festooned horns). Other ornamental details include bands of anthemion and acanthus leaves, favorite classical motifs.

Solomon Cordwell Buenz & Associates
646 North Michigan Avenue
1990

Crate & Barrel's flagship store is distinguished by its low-scale, sleek alternating horizontal bands of glass and shiny white aluminum, and a full-height, glass-enclosed corner rotunda. Escalators were placed in the transparent rotunda to maximize merchandising space on the small site and to draw customers to its upper floors; during the crowded holiday season, passengers seem to glide from floor to floor like colorful ribbons. The curved corner element becomes the fulcrum of the plan, radiating along both Michigan Avenue and Erie Street, reminiscent of Louis Sullivan's Carson Pirie Scott store at the corner of State and Madison Streets in the Loop. Although the exterior contrasts in color and material with the masonry Woman's Athletic Club next door (see #38), both buildings are similar in height, so a street wall continuity is maintained. Such low-scale development is especially welcome, given the huge towers that have been developed on Michigan Avenue since the late 1960s. The interior, designed in cooperation with Ray Arenson of Crate & Barrel, is sheathed in light knotty pine to convey a neutral background for the clean, modern home products displayed here.

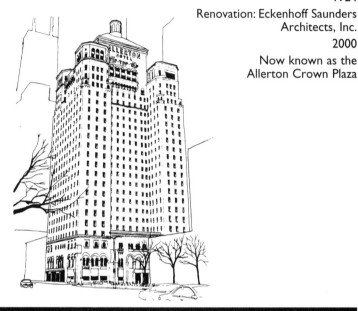

Murgatroyd and Ogden
Associate Architects, Fugard and Knapp
701 North Michigan Avenue
1924
Renovation: Eckenhoff Saunders
Architects, Inc.
2000
Now known as the
Allerton Crown Plaza

Built in the North Italian Renaissance style, with a central tower flanked by four smaller towers and a series of arched windows and corbeled sills, this 25-story building was among the first to be completed on North Michigan Avenue and was under construction at the same time as the nearby Tribune Tower (see #33). Although the shaft of the hotel is red brick, its three-story limestone base harmonizes with other limestone buildings that were being built or planned for the new avenue. Ground-floor retail space is on the Michigan Avenue side while the two-story, triple-arched entrance is on Huron Street. Inside, a grand two-story limestone stairwell continues the stylistic theme. Modeled on the Barbizon Hotel and other Allerton "Clubs" that catered to young professional men and women, the building combined the amenities of a private club and a hotel. For instance, it originally had a rooftop eighteen-hole golf course and handball court, workout rooms on every floor, a library, weekly dancing and card parties, and even an Allerton Glee Club. Fourteen floors were designated for men and six floors for women, who used a separate elevator bank. The building was renovated in 2000 as a hotel.

John Ronan Architects
61 West Superior Street
2011

In 2009, a stunning $100 million bequest from heiress Ruth Lilly gave *Poetry* magazine, founded in 1912 by poet Harriet Monroe, the opportunity to build itself a permanent home. An architectural competition ensued, won by Chicagoan John Ronan (b. 1964). His scheme suggests metaphors related to the art of poetry while meeting programmatic requirements including exhibition and performance space, a library, Foundation offices and a garden. The small, two-story, 26,000-square-foot building is set in a dense downtown neighborhood on an L-shaped lot. A corrugated, oxidized zinc screen, perforated where it screens the garden from the street, defines the site. To reach the building entrance, one must walk the length of the garden area, in which single trees are staggered with slivers of moss and set in a scored concrete ground. Visible to the right, sheathed in glass, is the double-height library. Its bookshelves provide not only substance but also color. To the left past the narrow gallery area is an enclosed performance room acoustically attuned for the spoken word. Furniture, bookshelves, and details throughout are made of Baltic fir. Unlike many dramatic designs that focus on form, the Poetry Foundation celebrates what lies within: a sophisticated interplay of space, materials, color, and light.

This mixed-use building of pink Swedish granite is among several designed by Skidmore, Owings & Merrill on North Michigan Avenue (see #48 and #53). It combines the low-rise, four-story Neiman Marcus Department Store facing Michigan Avenue and a 63-story tower with office and residential use configured on a north/south axis and entered on Chicago Avenue. The height of the Michigan Avenue section respects the context and memory of a lower-scale street, where wide sidewalks and ground-floor retail encourage pedestrian use. Notable is the grand two-story entrance arch; though non–load bearing, it recalls the language of such Chicago School buildings as the Rookery and the Auditorium Building (see #6). Its "keystone" is a glass slit connecting to an arched skylight. Note the coffered underside of the arch, with its backlit, translucent glass. The tapering of the tower results from the greater size requirements for office space, while the 200 condominiums above have smaller floorplates but larger windows. Architect Adrian Smith (b. 1944) is known for his evocative interpretations of the past, which are blended with state-of-the-art structural systems, here developed by engineer and SOM partner, Fazlur Khan.

W. W. Boyington

800 North Michigan Avenue; 163 East Pearson Street

1867–9

Renovation:
Morris Architects/Planners
2002–3

The Water Tower was the pride of Chicago when completed in 1869, housing the technology required to provide an adequate water supply to the growing young city in a dignified "castellated Gothic" structure. The tower contained the 138-foot standpipe needed to equalize the pressure of the eighteen million gallons of water pumped daily from the squat pumping station on the east side of Michigan Avenue. Naively Gothic in form, the tower rises from a foursquare plan with identical façades, corner turrets, crenellated battlements, and slit windows. Note the crude window architraves and the contrast of the tower's green copper cap with the sunny rusticated limestone from Joliet, Illinois. When the water tower survived the Chicago Fire of 1871, it became a symbol of the city's rebuilding spirit and energy. Indeed, the planners who widened Pine Street in 1918 to create the new North Michigan Avenue angled the street's path to sidestep these structures. The tower became functionally obsolete long ago, but has been preserved and serves today as a visitor information center. The pumping station still pumps water for the central city. In 2002, its interior space was renovated to become the new home of the Lookinglass Theater.

Josef Paul Kleihues
234 East Chicago Ave.
1996

The five-story, 151,000-square-foot Museum of Contemporary Art by German architect Josef Paul Kleihues (b. 1933) is five times the size of the museum's former home. Its one-acre sculpture garden takes advantage of the spectacular site overlooking Lake Michigan just east of the historic Chicago Water Tower (see #43) that survived the 1871 Chicago Fire. One of the most striking features of Chicago's newest museum is its soaring 56-foot-high glass-fronted façade, which is set above a sixteen-foot base of Indiana limestone and provides views of two levels of the interior. Also unusual are the hand-cast aluminum panels fastened with stainless steel buttons to the façade. The ground floor houses support space, a 15,000-square-foot education center, and the museum store. Two-story-high gallery spaces on the second floor house temporary exhibitions. Another level of galleries, located on the fourth floor, includes barrel-vaulted skylights and is devoted primarily to the museum's permanent collection. A restaurant and special events space run the width of the building's eastern façade, with views of the sculpture garden and Lake Michigan beyond.

Ludwig Mies van der Rohe
Associate Architects: Pace Associates;
Holsman, Holsman, Klekamp and Taylor
1949–51

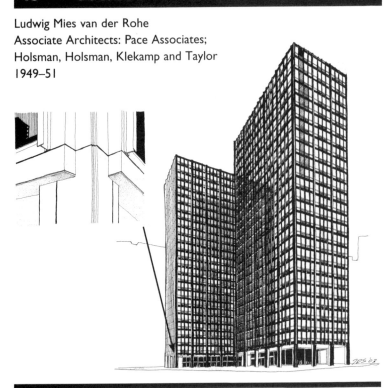

For more than 50 years they have stood as icons of modernity, the twin 26-story glass and steel apartment towers on Lake Shore Drive facing Lake Michigan. Here, the internal skeleton and the external design are one and the whole is sheathed in panes of glass. Consider the buildings as one composition with the long sides set at right angles to each other and connected by a canopy. Placed masterfully on the trapezoidal site, the buildings face both each other and the city's edge. The towers are based on a 21-foot module, the width of each bay. The long sides are five bays across; the short sides are three bays across. Each bay is further divided into four parts, with the center sections nine inches wider than the outer sides. Verticality is emphasized by steel I-beams welded to the exterior surface, since the structural steel columns themselves had to be covered in concrete to meet Chicago's building code. At the base, the buildings seem to rise on their tiptoes and the resulting freestanding columns form an arcade providing additional light, air, and views. As a young architect in Germany, Mies had imagined steel and glass towers in a series of sketches begun in 1919. Thirty years later his ideas were realized in Chicago.

This mixed-use structure combines a seven-story vertical shopping mall, office space, the Ritz-Carlton Hotel lobby area, and a 62-story, 859-foot tower that contains hotel rooms and 200 condominiums. The shopping mall has a large atrium with glass elevators rising dramatically through it. Over 100 shops as well as restaurants and theaters are contained within its 610,000 square feet. To maximize rentable space, the mall has blank walls above the ground-floor windows, turning its back on one of Chicago's great streets. At street level, however, its escalators are visible though the ground-floor windows, funneling consumers to its treasures within. The mixed-use program, seen also in Olympia Centre (see #42), One Magnificent Mile (see #53), and 900 North Michigan Avenue (see #51), is still searching for its form. Here, a low-scale box is attached to a tower behind it. Once considered a daring venture, since it brought a suburban mall concept to the heart of the city, the interior shopping area has precedents in Chicago in several nineteenth-century skyscrapers that were organized around interior atria as well as the more recent, but now destroyed, Diana Court in Holabird and Root's Michigan Square Building (1928).

Ralph Adams Cram
126 East Chestnut Street
1912–4
Manse, Parish House, Cloister, and Blair Chapel
Howard Van Doren Shaw, 1925
Gratz Center, Gensler, 2012

The first Presbyterian congregation in Chicago was organized in 1833, the same year Chicago became a town. The Fourth Presbyterian Church represents a consolidation of various congregations and was built on land made available by the McCormicks, wealthy church parishioners. When it opened in 1914, North Michigan Avenue, then called Pine Street, was little more than a dirt road along the marshy shoreline, and the church overlooked Lake Michigan instead of the John Hancock Center (see #48). Ralph Adams Cram (1862–1945), architect of the Cathedral of St. John the Divine in New York City, designed this church in the English Perpendicular Gothic style, with its requisite carved ornament: crockets on the arches, spire, and pinnacle, quatrefoils and cinquefoils in the window tracery. The building is uniform in plan and constructed of gray Bedford limestone; its verticality is emphasized by its 122-foot spire and by the narrow lancet windows of its belfry. The façade of the sanctuary is composed of two monumental compound pointed arches, the lower housing the double entrance doors, the upper framing a large stained glass window. Adjacent to the church and connected to it by an ivy-covered cloister are the parish house and manse, designed by Howard Van Doren Shaw, complementing the church.

Like a giant bridge set on its side, the 100-story John Hancock Center is marked by huge X-braces that stiffen the structure against wind forces while forming a distinctive pattern on its surface. Controversial from the start for its enormous hulk and dark metal cladding, this mixed-use project, combining retail, residential, and office space, broke all the rules of its genteel, mostly low-rise Michigan Avenue neighborhood. It was soon celebrated for its very brashness, however, becoming a Chicago icon complete with a nickname: "Big John." Engineer Fazlur Khan (1929–82), working with architect Bruce Graham, devised the ingenious "braced tube" system, carrying loads downward so efficiently that only 29.7 pounds of steel per square foot were required, a third less than in comparable buildings. These exterior tubes support the structure, necessitating no interior columns. The building occupies only 50 percent of its full-block site; a plaza on Michigan Avenue occupies the other half, providing an open space for pedestrians and a showcase for the skyscraper. A recent renovation has revitalized the street and concourse levels by clarifying entrances and creating inviting spaces for relaxing and dining.

Jean Paul Viguier
20 East Chestnut Street
1999–2002

This 32-story hotel creates its striking presence in part by absence. Imagine you have four wooden geometrical shapes: a triangular wedge, an elliptical cone, a vertical post, and a rectangular box. Jean-Paul Viguier (b. 1946), an internationally distinguished French modern architect, started with a great wedge for the guest room tower, the hypotenuse of which faces Wabash Avenue. He then sliced the entire edge of the wedge with an imaginary elliptical cone of the same height, whose peak is at the top of the building. The cone is subtracted, but its curve remains. This maneuver indents the full face of the corner—where not one of the windows is the same size—curves the lower section where the Café des Architectes resides, and creates an elliptical plaza at street level. As for the remaining shapes: the vertical post is used for mechanical and other services at the rear, and the rectangular box forms the lobby and public space. On the stone exterior, Viguier uses several versions of window modules rather than lines of static fenestration. The interior by Pierre-Yves Rochon is deluxe elegance. Viguier, who received a master's degree in City Planning from Harvard University, is involved in a variety of projects from designing the Parc Citröen in Paris to planning a "New Town" in Malaysia for a population of 650,000.

Holabird and Root
919 North Michigan Avenue
1927–9
Now known by its address

Six symmetrical setbacks sculpt the mass of this 37-story Indiana limestone high-rise that once dominated the vista on Michigan Avenue north
of the Chicago River. The site, a mile north of the Loop business district,
was selected by the Palm-Olive-Peet Company because of its dramatic
lakefront views and prestigious surroundings adjacent to the residential Gold Coast. Vertical piers alternate with recessed, window-filled
channels, creating a regular rhythm on the façade that carries the eye
upward. Exterior decoration is limited to incised designs on piers and
entrances. Lighting is another key element of the Art Deco style; here,
electrical floodlights emphasize the powerful setbacks. For over 50 years
it had a powerful beacon on its rooftop to guide aerial and maritime
traffic; eventually it became a nuisance as other towers arose nearby.
Combining grace and power with masterful planning on an exceptional
site, this structure is considered among the best of Holabird and Root's
work. John Augur Holabird (1886–1945) and John Wellborn Root, Jr.
(1887–1963) were sons of prominent Chicago architects John Holabird
(1854–1923) and John Wellborn Root (1850–91). They joined the firm
Holabird and Roche in 1919, renaming it Holabird and Root upon the
death of the senior partners.

Kohn Pedersen Fox
Associate Architects, Perkins & Will
1983–9

Among the largest mixed-use projects on Michigan Avenue, this building adheres to the box-plus-tower concept to address its complex programmatic requirements of retail, office, hotel, condominium, and parking facilities. Like its sister center Water Tower Place (see #46), developed a decade earlier, the vertical retail mall is contained in an eight-story cube that preserves the low-scale character of Michigan Avenue at street level. Above, its setback tower is a sentinel for the view north on the Avenue, much as 333 North Michigan Avenue is to the south, creating both a personality and an identity for their portions of the famous street. The structural engineering of this building combines two systems: steel for the lower twenty stories of retail and office sections and a concrete tube above, which allows more open floor plates. The retail base contains the interior shopping mall, including Bloomingdale's, for which the retail complex is named. Above the base are the Four Seasons Hotel guest room floors, office floors, and residential apartments. The entrance is marked by a huge round portal through which are views of the shopping atrium, and the top is crowned with four corner pavilions and lanterns.

Marshall and Fox
140 East Walton Street
1919

Overlooking Oak Street Beach, where the residential Gold Coast meets fashionable North Michigan Avenue, the 800-room Drake Hotel represents subdued elegance and comfort. Inspired by Italian Renaissance palazzos, architects Benjamin Marshall and Charles Fox punctuated the sheer limestone walls with regularly spaced windows and Renaissance decorative motifs such as consoles and garlands. The main reception rooms are located, Italian-style, on a *piano nobile*, and windows here are capped by alternating round and flattened arches. Above the Lake Shore Drive entrance, a colonnade connects the two side wings; inside is a two-story grand ballroom with oversized columns. The Drake, designed in an H-shaped block to maximize exterior views, offered large family apartment units, an entire floor for bachelors, and first-class accommodations. Completed just before the opening of the Michigan Avenue Bridge in 1920, it was among the first buildings constructed on the new thoroughfare that replaced narrow Pine Street, which was broadened and renamed North Michigan Avenue. Its developers, John B. and Tracy C. Drake earlier developed the Blackstone Hotel (see #3), also designed by Marshall and Fox, as was the Lake Shore Trust and Savings Bank (see #37).

One Magnificent Mile is a showcase of the possibilities of the bundled-tube structural system, pioneered by the talented team of engineer Fazlur Khan and architect Bruce Graham. Khan was a partner at Skidmore, Owings & Merrill, and one of the country's most innovative structural engineers. He collaborated with Graham on the John Hancock Center (see #48) and the Sears Tower (1974), and with Adrian Smith on Olympia Centre (see #42). Here, three hexagonal concrete tubes with punched window openings rise 57, 49, and 21 stories, respectively, and are joined as a bundled tube to resist wind loads. The perimeter tubes eliminated structural cores, allowing uninterrupted floorspans. Residential condominiums are above the two-story mechanical floors at the 21-story line; offices are below, with retail on the first three levels. The distinctive shape was chosen in order to meet several criteria: maximizing size while minimizing shadows that would fall on nearby Oak Street Park Beach; relating to other neighboring buildings, as befits a corner site; and creating a distinctive gateway to the city's prestigious retail corridor. For example, note how its six-story sloped entrance nods toward the Drake Hotel across Michigan Avenue (see #52) instead of overwhelming it with taller elements at the street edge.

The Loop

CHICAGO
RIVER

RANDOLPH

WASHINGTON

MADISON

MONROE

ADAMS

JACKSON

VAN BUREN

CONGRESS PKWY.

HARRISON

POLK

HALSTED

KENNEDY EXPRESSWAY

SOUTH DESPLAINES

JEFFERSON

CLINTON

CANAL

WACKER

FRANKLIN

WELLS

LASALLE

CLARK

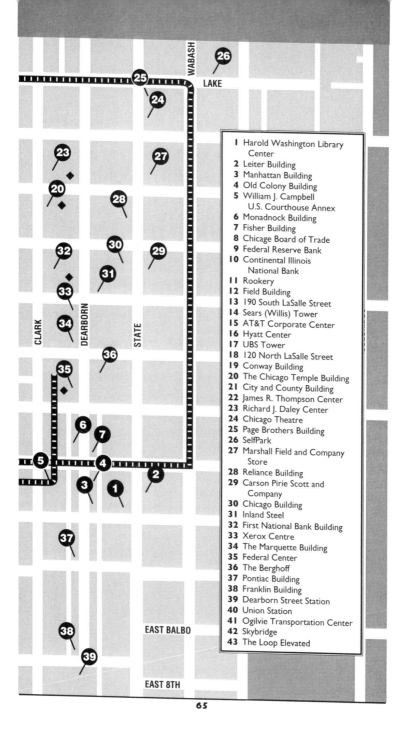

WABASH

LAKE

1 Harold Washington Library Center
2 Leiter Building
3 Manhattan Building
4 Old Colony Building
5 William J. Campbell U.S. Courthouse Annex
6 Monadnock Building
7 Fisher Building
8 Chicage Board of Trade
9 Federal Reserve Bank
10 Continental Illinois National Bank
11 Rookery
12 Field Building
13 190 South LaSalle Street
14 Sears (Willis) Tower
15 AT&T Corporate Center
16 Hyatt Center
17 UBS Tower
18 120 North LaSalle Street
19 Conway Building
20 The Chicago Temple Building
21 City and County Building
22 James R. Thompson Center
23 Richard J. Daley Center
24 Chicago Theatre
25 Page Brothers Building
26 SelfPark
27 Marshall Field and Company Store
28 Reliance Building
29 Carson Pirie Scott and Company
30 Chicago Building
31 Inland Steel
32 First National Bank Building
33 Xerox Centre
34 The Marquette Building
35 Federal Center
36 The Berghoff
37 Pontiac Building
38 Franklin Building
39 Dearborn Street Station
40 Union Station
41 Ogilvie Transportation Center
42 Skybridge
43 The Loop Elevated

CLARK   DEARBORN   STATE

EAST BALBO

EAST 8TH

Hammond, Beeby and Babka

Full block bounded by State Street, Congress Parkway, Plymouth Court, and Van Buren Street

1989–91

Named in honor of Chicago's first black mayor, Harold Washington, this ten-story, 756,640-square-foot red granite and brick building is the largest public library in the United States. Its Postmodern design won a highly publicized architectural competition in 1988 and recalls significant Chicago School of Architecture buildings: the three-story rusticated stone base reflects the Rookery (see #11), the deeply recessed arched windows are inspired by the nearby Auditorium Building, and the sloping brick midsection recalls the Monadnock Building (see #6). As in the City and County Building (see #21), the building's civic nature is identified by the monumental scale of its elements. Further, Chicago iconography enlivens the façade: Ceres, goddess of grain, wears a necklace of corn tied with a ribbon inscribed with the city's motto, "Urbs in Horto," while above, festoons are anchored by medallions with the Chicago River "Y" and a "Windy City" head. Administrative offices and a wintergarden occupy the top floor, where intersecting metal and glass barrel vaults offer natural light and structural drama. Service facilities are located on the perimeter of the glass-sided west wall facing Plymouth Court. The building interior is arranged on a generous 21-foot column grid, providing flexibility for the library's changing needs.

William Le Baron Jenney
403 South State Street
1891
Now known as the Second Leiter Building

Occupying a full block at Congress Parkway and State Street, the eight-story, 553,000-square-foot Second Leiter Building was advertised as the largest retail establishment in the world when completed. It was an excellent investment for Levi Z. Leiter, who in 1881 left his partnership with merchandiser Marshall Field to become a real estate developer. The building was first leased to Siegel, Cooper and Company; Sears, Roebuck and Company occupied it 1932–1978. Though William Le Baron Jenney (1832–1907) developed a successful architectural practice in Chicago, he was trained as a civil engineer and served with the Union Army Corps of Engineers during the Civil War. Some historians consider this building Jenney's most successful work because the clarity of its design matches his engineering skill. The well-proportioned gray Maine granite façade is a straightforward expression of the underlying steel grid. Smooth, slender piers stretch the eye upward and give the building lightness; wide horizontal glass expanses let the large mass breathe. Minimal interior columns and sixteen-foot ceilings created open floors where merchandise could be effectively displayed. Thus the building met the needs of the architectural program while creating an aesthetically pleasing composition.

William Le Baron Jenney
431 South Dearborn Street
1889–91; Renovation: Hasbrouck-Hunderman
1982

William Le Baron Jenney's office was a center for young architects who came to Chicago to rebuild the city after the 1871 fire: Louis Sullivan, William Holabird, Daniel Burnham, and Martin Roche all apprenticed there. Jenney is best known for his Home Insurance Company Building (1885, destroyed), which first used the steel skeleton frame to support an exterior wall. His Manhattan Building illustrates the integration of several additional technological innovations that made further development of the modern skyscraper possible. First, since the structure was sandwiched between two smaller buildings, he had to lessen the loads on the party walls. To do so, he set the Manhattan Building back at the tenth floor, thus designing the first setback skyscraper. Second, he adapted knee and portal bracing from bridge construction to gird the building against the wind. Third, he developed a system of hangers to attach the masonry units to the frame of each floor, allowing them to shift with the movement of the skeleton frame. Thus, although the confused façade reflects uncertainty about the appropriate exterior expression for this new building type, many elements of today's skyscrapers are already addressed in this early commercial high-rise.

Holabird and Roche
407 South Dearborn Street
1893–4

The Old Colony stands among a distinguished group of early skyscrapers along South Dearborn Street: the Manhattan Building, the Monadnock Building, and the Fisher Building. There are no masonry bearing walls in this building, and the internal structure of the building is visible in the window grid pattern on the broad limestone façades along Dearborn Street and Plymouth Court. On the building's shorter sides, Chicago windows are flanked by double-hung windows in a rhythm punctuated by the rounded bay windows that wrap around the corners to admit additional light and air to the building. The Old Colony's seventeen-story height required a wind-bracing system that includes four sets of portal arches that extend from the foundation to the roof and brace the horizontal and vertical structural elements. Built on speculation by Boston lawyer Francis Bartlett, the building was named for the first English colony in America at Plymouth, Massachusetts. Note its seal carved in stone at the entrance. The building was a successful venture, offering 600 offices that were occupied by railroad, printing, and lumber interests who sought space here in the thriving printing center of the Midwest.

Harry Weese and Associates
71 West Van Buren Street
1973–5

This 27-story reinforced concrete tower, also known as the Metropolitan Correctional Center, was planned for those awaiting trial on federal charges and is unique in several respects. Detention centers are rarely placed in business district locations or housed in skyscrapers. Yet Harry Weese's (1915–98) inventive design accommodates both the rigorous program requirements necessary to house inmates and the context of the historic south Loop location. The triangular configuration minimizes corridor lengths for guards while providing maximum perimeter space for windows, each of which is five inches wide, the largest allowed by Bureau of Prison standards. These openings form an interesting, computer-punch-card-like abstract pattern on the smooth façade. Lower floors function as administrative and social service areas, while the upper levels are for inmates. Each multipurpose core space serves 44 people and is divided into a two-story unit, with inmates' rooms arranged around common lounge, dining, and visitors' facilities. In good weather, note the inmates using the roof-top exercise yard. At the building's base, the landscaped plaza creates an inviting entrance typical of many office buildings in the area. Original and efficient, this building is among Weese's most thoughtful designs.

Northern half: Burnham and Root
Southern half: Holabird and Roche
53 West Jackson Boulevard
Northern half, 1891;
southern half, 1893

Initially planned as four connected buildings, the Monadnock Building, in its unadorned functionalism, embodies Chicago commercial architecture. It was developed on a narrow 400- by 68-foot lot by Bostonians Peter and Shepherd Brooks, with Owen Aldis as their Chicago agent, and is named after Mount Monadnock in New Hampshire. In the northern section, John Root (1850–91) of Burnham & Root, who had also designed the Rookery for the Brooks brothers, maximized rentable space by stretching the building to an unheard-of sixteen stories and punching out a grid of bay windows that also added light and ventilation. To support this height, exterior masonry walls six feet thick at the base were required. Note how the curve of the corners is repeated in the cavetto cornice. After Root's death in 1891, the firm of Holabird and Roche was hired to develop the southern half of the block. Here, in the last quadrant, the building is supported by the new steel frame construction, rather than the old-fashioned masonry bearing wall. Thus, in this massive block, constructed over a period of three years, we can see the end of one era in construction and the beginning of another.

D. H. Burnham and Co.
343 South Dearborn Street
1895–6; addition, 1906

The eighteen-story Fisher Building was among the tallest commercial structures in the world when it was completed in 1896. Charles Atwood (1840–95) is credited with the design, Edward Shankland (1854–1924), with the construction. The building combines inventive structural solutions with fanciful ornament. Steel columns were riveted together to form continuous rigid supports, an efficient construction method that allowed the entire frame to be erected in a month. The foundation required to support such a tall building on Chicago's swampy soil presented another challenge. The solution was to drive groups of massive piles 40 feet underground surmounted by a pyramid of I-beams laid in cross section and filled with Portland cement. The exterior reveals a distinctive interplay between glass and rich golden terra cotta ornament. Note the playful marine shapes on the lower floors that refer to the building's owner, Lucius G. Fisher, while above, whimsical creatures creep and slither along Gothic arches and window sills, evidence of Atwood's exuberant imagination. Terra cotta was also used inside the building, where it sheaths the flat steel arches supporting the floors. The three-bay addition to the north was designed by Peter J. Weber (1864–1923), also of Burnham's office.

Holabird and Root
141 West Jackson Boulevard
1929–30
Addition: Murphy/Jahn with
Shaw and Associates and
Swanke, Hayden, Connell Architects
1980

The Chicago Board of Trade stands in the center of LaSalle Street, at once proclaiming the centrality of nature's bounty to Chicago's economy and the human ability to abstract nature into a sophisticated trading mechanism. The first Board of Trade on this site was designed by W. W. Boyington (1818–98) in 1885. The present structure is a 45-story limestone Art Deco skyscraper, for a quarter century the tallest building in Chicago. Thirty-story wings flank the nine-story base, above which rises a central clock adorned with Alvin Meyer's sculpted allegorical figures: a hooded figure for wheat and an Indian with corn, representing the grains of the Old World and the New. John Storr's aluminum Ceres, goddess of agriculture, tops the metal pyramidal roof. The spacious two-story interior of the lobby is detailed with scalloped curves, metal banding, and dramatic lighting. Fifty years after the building's completion another trading floor was needed, as well as new offices for the Chicago commodities exchange. Architect Helmut Jahn's (b. 1940) 24-story addition reinterprets the original building's massing in glass and steel. Note John Warner Norton's mural of Ceres that once graced the original trading floor and now hangs in the addition's spectacular twelve-story atrium.

Graham, Anderson, Probst and White
230 South LaSalle Street
1920–2
Southwestern addition: Naess and Murphy, 1957;
northwestern addition: Holabird and Root, 1984–9

Dignified and imposing, the sixteen-story limestone Federal Reserve Bank houses the Chicago branch of the central banking system. Together with its "twin" across the street (see #10), it forms a symmetrical end to LaSalle Street at the Chicago Board of Trade (see #8). Six massive Corinthian columns topped by a pediment mark the LaSalle Street entrance. Above them the exterior is plain, but the interior is not. Its grand three-story banking hall was renovated by Holabird and Root in the 1980s and opened to the street level to provide a spectacular four-level entrance lobby. The renovation also included a fourteen-story addition on the northwest corner of the site, a new limestone cladding on the 1957 addition, and a complete reorganization of the building's internal work and traffic flow. In addition to office space, the building also includes banking and check processing operations, warehousing, and safekeeping areas. This structure was one of seven Federal Reserve Bank buildings designed by Graham, Anderson, Probst and White during the 1920s, evidence of the firm's ability to provide expressive form for America's financial establishment.

Graham, Anderson, Probst and White
231 South LaSalle Street
1923–4
Formerly known as the
Illinois Merchants
Bank Building

The Federal Reserve Bank (see #9) and the Continental Illinois National Bank directly across LaSalle Street were designed by the same firm and share many similarities: massing, proportions, materials, and the style so often associated with financial institutions, the dignified Greek temple. Here, the entrance is marked by six Ionic columns supporting the pediment, while, on the interior, twenty-eight Ionic columns line the magnificent two-story banking room that stretches across the entire length of the building on the second floor. Note the murals painted by Jules Guerin (1866–1946), perhaps best known for his renderings that accompanied Daniel H. Burnham's 1909 Plan of Chicago. Graham, Anderson, Probst and White was the second successor firm to D. H. Burnham and Company. When Daniel Burnham died in 1912, Ernest Graham (1868–1936) assumed leadership of the prolific firm known for its Beaux Arts aesthetic and large-scale projects. Peirce Anderson (1870–1924), Edward Probst (1870–1942), and Howard Judson White (1870–1936) joined him as partners five years later. In Chicago, their work includes such landmarks as The Wrigley Building, the Merchandise Mart and Union Station (see #40).

Burnham and Root
209 South LaSalle Street
1885–8
Lobby renovation: Frank Lloyd Wright, 1905; William Drummond, 1931
Restoration: Hasbrouck-Hunderman, 1983; McClier Corporation, 1989–92

Nicknamed for the birds that roosted in the temporary City Hall that had occupied this site, the twelve-story Rookery combines structural and mechanical innovations with a sophisticated aesthetic. Designer John Wellborn Root, trained as an engineer, was challenged to support the enormous bulk of this building on Chicago's marshy soil. He devised a new foundation system, called "floating foundations," concrete rafts interleaved with iron rails for added strength. The architects, experimenting with steel-frame technology, employed a metal frame for the Quincy Court side of the building, but the rest of the Rookery uses traditional bearing-wall construction. The robust Romanesque exterior has a two-story rusticated granite base punctuated by glass and stone columns, a grand arched entry (note the two rooks), and intricate terra cotta ornament. But the Rookery's interior is its glory: a two-story glass-roofed atrium supported by an iron frame, providing maximum light to interior offices while creating a dynamic spatial experience. Note the curving, cantilevered oriel staircase, with its carved Moorish details. Twenty years after the atrium's completion, Frank Lloyd Wright (1867–1959) modernized the space by replacing much of the delicate ironwork with gold-incised white marble.

Graham, Anderson, Probst and White
135 South LaSalle Street
1928–34

Located on the site of William Le Baron Jenney's Home Insurance Building (often considered the first skyscraper), the Field Building was an ambitious, speculative venture developed by the Marshall Field Estate trustees during the Great Depression. The modern, luxurious, million-square-foot office building was designed to offer first-class office space while symbolizing faith in Chicago's future. Designed by Alfred P. Shaw (1895–1970), the exterior is simple and elegant: four 22-story wings surround a central 43-story shaft sheathed in Indiana limestone. The shaft's skyward thrust is emphasized by recessed spandrels and soaring setbacks. The Clark and LaSalle Street entrances, connected by one of Chicago's few block-through arcades, are dressed with sleek Art Moderne motifs, such as stylized lettering and incised white bronze zigzags set in polished black granite. The Art Moderne style continues in the two-story lobby, where indirect lighting highlights distinctive nickel silver metalwork, high-speed elevators are monitored by the giant elevator indicator, and the main mail chute is cast in a bronze relief of the Field Building itself. Technologically advanced for its day, it was the last building built in the Loop until the construction of the Inland Steel building (see #31) twenty years later.

John Burgee with Philip Johnson
1983–7

This 40-story office building of red granite was inspired by John Wellborn Root's 22-story Masonic Temple Building of 1892 that stood on the northeast corner of Randolph and State until it was destroyed in 1939. Like the Masonic Temple Building, 190 South LaSalle has arches that stretch up the façade, culminating in pairs of distictive, two-story crested gables. A huge multi-use complex for its time, the Masonic Temple Building had a full-height atrium, a rooftop garden and promenade, and ten floors of shopping, restaurants, offices, and other facilities. As a speculative office building, 190 South LaSalle's programmatic requirements were simpler. However, its sumptuous gold-leaf barrel-vaulted lobby still recalls the grandeur of the past. The building exemplifies Postmodernism, a style or attitude that moves away from abstraction and toward reinterpreting representational forms, often drawing upon connections to the past. Although architect John Burgee (b. 1933) grew up in the Chicago area and practiced here before joining Philip Johnson (1906–2005) in New York, 190 South LaSalle is his first major office building completed in Chicago. By recalling a demolished historic building, it extends the memory of Root's work, while connecting itself to Chicago's remarkable design tradition.

Skidmore, Owings & Merrill
233 South Wacker Drive
1968–74; entrance addition, 1984–5
Renovation: DeStefano + Partners, 1992–3
Now known as the Willis Tower

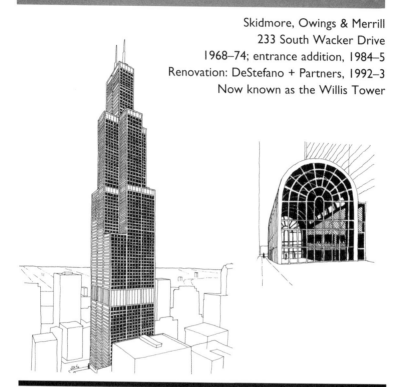

At 110 stories and 1,454 feet high, the Willis Tower is among the tallest buildings in the world. To ensure stability, a system of 75-foot-square structural tubes is used to act as perimeter columns, bracing the skyscraper against powerful wind forces. Nine of these huge tubes form the building's base. As the building rises, the number of tubes is reduced where setbacks occur: at the fiftieth, sixty-sixth, and ninetieth floors. Two tubes remain to support the tower, while steel columns comprising the building's frame serve to channel wind shear and gravity stress down to bedrock caissons. Design partner Bruce Graham (1925–2010) and engineer Fazlur Khan (1929–82) led the project team for this immense undertaking. It both symbolized Sears, Roebuck and Company's position as the largest retailer in the world and consolidated the company's offices. With its dark angular silhouette, the Sears Tower soon became a Chicago icon, but it was forbidding at street level. Several years ago, Skidmore, Owings & Merrill returned to design a vaulted atrium as a friendlier entrance and to renovate the lobby. More recently, work by DeStefano + Partners has created a more inviting lobby and better tourist access.

Skidmore, Owings and Merrill
227 West Monroe Street
1985–9
Now known as Franklin Center

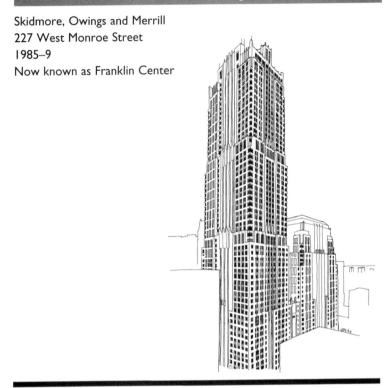

Architect Adrian Smith (b. 1944) sought to integrate the AT&T Corporate Center into the existing urban context by drawing upon the Art Moderne aesthetic of the 1920s, as seen in the Chicago Board of Trade (see #8) and the Field Building (see #12). Note the strong verticality of the AT&T Corporate Center's tripartite façade, with its recessed central plane, setbacks at the thirtieth, forty-fifth, and fifty-ninth floors, and stylized decorative details. The complex comprises two granite towers connected by an arcade from Monroe to Adams Street. The 60-story AT&T tower is polished red granite at the base, with lighter shades above, and its window spandrels are clad with 2,600 silkscreened dark-green aluminum panels. To relate such a large mass to the human scale, Smith placed a cornice line at the fifth story. The 4,000-square-foot lobby is one of the finest in the city; marble and fine woods are used to create intricate patterns. The second tower is 34 stories high and topped with a hipped roof. The complex creates an interesting dynamic and a sharp contrast to the Willis Tower nearby.

Pei Cobb Freed & Partners
Associate Architects:
A. Epstein & Sons
71 South Wacker Drive
2002–5

Perhaps the most obvious feature of this 48-story tower is its shape: a large oval from top to bottom, with the southern curve facing Monroe Street. Responding to a request from the major tenant, design architect Henry Cobb (b. 1926) eliminated corners to allow for more equal office sizes, creating this boat-like form. Cobb, a founding partner of the highly successful New York firm, Pei Cobb Freed & Partners, is well known as an educator as well as a designer. He served as Chairman of the Architecture Department at the Graduate School of Design at Harvard, his alma mater, and has worked on such projects as the John Hancock Tower in Boston and the Credit Suisse First Boston Tower at Canary Wharf in London. Much attention is given to how this 1,765,000-square-foot steel and glass tower meets the street. On the ground floor of the interior, a linear grove of bamboo lines the windows. Outside, the south and east sides of the skyscraper are recessed and landscaped with a public garden, including tear-drop planters at each end, a pleasing pedestrian amenity. Peter Lindsay Schaudt Landscape Architecture, Inc., which also landscaped the courtyards for State Street Village at the Illinois Institute of Technology (see Campus Architecture, #10), is responsible for the design.

Lohan Caprile Goettsch Architects
One North Wacker Drive
1999–2002

As the first speculative office tower to be constructed in Chicago since 1992, this 53-story, 1,300,000-square-foot skyscraper designed by James Goettsch (b. 1941) included oodles of amenities to attract tenants. And it worked: midway through construction, the Union Bank of Switzerland leased most of the space. Among the high-tech features are multiple shafts or risers for telecommunication wires, a rooftop communications and satellite system, and capacity for redundant energy and cooling systems. What most people see, however, is the striking block-long lobby facing Madison Street that is enclosed by an orthogonal web of 5- by 5-foot glass panels held in place by pre-stressed cables fastened by corner buttons. It is the first such system constructed in the United States, and since the glass used has a very low iron content, the hanging wall is nearly transparent. Outside, huge sidewalk granite planters of trees and mounds of green, designed by Peter Walker and Partners, provide color, shade, and sitting space. The exterior is composed of blue-tinted glass and stainless steel ribs joined at the perimeter by steel columns. The east façade bulges slightly where setbacks occur at floors 19 and 34, reflecting the elevator bank heights.

Murphy/Jahn
1992

This 40-story mid-block building on an asymmetrical site presented several challenges to architect Helmut Jahn. For example, in order to provide maximum floorplate size, he placed all fixed elements in a side core of the building, a design not unlike that of the Inland Steel building (see #31); to enhance natural light and enlarge the view, he extended a curved glass bay over LaSalle Street, permitting views of the LaSalle Street canyon. In addition, penthouse offices are topped by the vaulting glass curved roof of the structure. The building's exterior skin is alternating bands of gray and white granite, a pattern repeated in the lobby floor. The focus of the lobby is artist Roger Brown's 20- by 50-foot mosaic of Daedalus, the mythical patron saint of architecture, who is shown escaping into the clouds with his son Icarus on wings fashioned of wax and feathers. On the ground floor, storefronts are suspended clear glass without vertical mullions, resulting in a transparent wall with a clear view of the interior lobby. Other Jahn designs in the Loop include One South Wacker Drive, the Xerox Centre (see #33), the Chicago Board of Trade addition (see #8), and the James R. Thompson Center (see #22).

D. H. Burnham and Co. and Graham, Burnham and Company
111 West Washington Street
1912–3
Now known as Burnham Center

Developed by the estate of Marshall Field and named after Field's birth-place, Conway, Massachusetts, this 21-story office building follows the prototype developed by the architectural firm D. H. Burnham and Co. at the turn of the century: a two-story glass atrium lobby, above which is a square open well to provide light and ventilation, and glazed white terra cotta sheathing, reflecting Burnham's wish to "lighten up" commercial buildings in the Loop. Classical detailing also recalls the influence of the 1893 World's Columbian Exposition, where the Beaux Arts aesthetic dominated. Note the Conway Building's rounded corners (typical of many nineteenth-century Loop buildings), and its unaltered three-story rooftop colonnade and elaborate balustrade. Frederick H. Dinkelberg (c. 1869–1935) of D. H. Burnham's office is credited with this design; when Burnham died in 1912, his successor firm, Graham, Burnham and Company, completed the project. When the building was purchased in 1944, the new owner filled in the interior court to the height of six stories to create more offices.

Holabird and Roche
77 West Washington
1922–3

Formerly the First
Methodist-Episcopal Church,
now the First United
Methodist Church

The tallest church in the world, the First United Methodist Church sits at the base of a 21-story commercial office tower. The building's entrances are separated according to purpose: Washington Street for the offices, Clark Street to reach the 1,500-seat sanctuary. Above the office block is an eight-story Gothic spire; its additional weight is distributed by a complex system of girders and bracing. Within the spire is the Chapel in the Sky and a rectory for the minister. At 556 feet, the building was more than twice Chicago's height limit of the time: 260 feet. Fortunately, the City Council granted a waiver of the ordinance before the building was completed. This valuable site is located diagonally across from the original Courthouse Square, now the site of the City and County Building (see #21), and has been owned by the church since 1845; far smaller church buildings preceded the present edifice. Today's economic and development pressures have led some churches to realize the value of their air rights by building skyscrapers that tower above their steeples. However, Holabird and Roche's solution kept the church's position intact, for in their design the spire, not the office tower, is closer to the heavens.

Holabird and Roche
Block bounded by LaSalle, Clark, Randolph, and Washington Streets
County Building, 1907; City Hall, 1911

In 1831, the Illinois legislature created Cook County, established Chicago as the county seat, and designated this block for a county courthouse that was built four years later. In 1848, John Mills Van Osdel (1811–91) designed the first city offices above the public market, straddling State Street north of Randolph. City and county government functions were first joined on the courthouse site in another building designed by Van Osdel in 1853. Chicago's explosive economic growth soon required enlarged governmental facilities. After the Chicago fire of 1871, a massive City Hall/County Building designed by James Egan (1839–1914) was finally completed in 1885, but was demolished twenty years later for the present structure. Here, Holabird and Roche's use of classical elements on a monumental scale defines the eleven-story gray granite structure as a public building. Note, for example, the majestic colonnade of six-story Corinthian columns, massive piers, and the 24-foot-high entablature. On the interior, the lobby walls are faced in Botticino marble, as are the ceiling vaults and main corridors on the upper floors. This City and County Building has now served local government for over a century, a testament to its functionality and symbolic civic virtues.

Murphy/Jahn with Lester B. Knight and Associates
Bounded by Randolph, LaSalle, Lake, and Clark Streets
1979–85
Formerly known as the State of Illinois Center

Has a spaceship landed in the Loop? Helmut Jahn's 1,150,000-square-foot State of Illinois Center, renamed the James R. Thompson Center to honor the former Illinois governor, is a daring polychrome design that reinterprets the classical forms and grammar of monumental public buildings. In a city renowned for its skyscrapers, this low, seventeen-story building makes an impact with its cylindrical shape, playful details, and spectacular skylit rotunda. Occupying a full city block, the structure follows the city grid on three sides, but pulls back at the southeast corner to form a curved entrance. Note sculptor Jean Dubuffet's (1901–85) *Monument with Standing Beast* (1984). The glass and steel exterior is divided into three tiers by setbacks, while the surface juxtaposes silver and blue vertical stripes with horizontal salmon bands. Like a great round eye, a modern-day dome rises from the edge of the roof at a 45-degree angle. At the concourse level, a spiral-patterned marble and granite floor emphasizes the curving interior space. Free-standing glass elevators and escalators leading to state offices are placed at the edge of the 160-foot-diameter rotunda. Although it carries noise and dirt into work areas, the openness was meant to symbolize government accessibility.

C. F. Murphy Associates; Skidmore, Owings and Merrill; and Loebl Schlossman and Bennett

Bounded by Washington, Randolph, Dearborn, and Clark Streets

1965

Formerly the Chicago Civic Center

Set on the north side of a great open plaza, the 31-story tower, designed by Jacques Brownson (1923–2012) of C. F. Murphy Associates, gives Chicago an extraordinary public space. The placement of the tower on the site opens the view to Holabird and Roche's Beaux Arts City and County Building (see #21), which provides a striking contrast to the Daley Center's structural grid of glass and steel. Yet they share the monumental proportions that mark public buildings in Chicago. For example, each of the Daley Center's three structural bays is 87 feet long and almost 48 feet wide, and the long spandrels are stretched across the façade like bridge girders. Note how the great rectangular columns, strongly rooted in the ground, become progressively thinner as they rise to the roof. The whole surface is integrated by the use of amber-tinted glass and Cor-Ten steel, which ages to a rich brown. Picasso's 50-foot-high sculpture is also of Cor-Ten steel and was the artist's gift to the city of Chicago. A modern sphinx, it hears the city at its feet: farmers' markets, political rallies, summertime music, and the latest deal.

Rapp and Rapp
175 North State Street
1921

The Chicago Theatre marquee is a Loop landmark and a symbol of the city. Note the City of Chicago's insignia: an encircled "Y," representing the three branches of the Chicago River. Built when cinema design was evolving from simple storefront nickelodeons showing silent pictures to the flamboyant movie theaters of the later 1920s, the 4,000-seat Chicago Theatre was one of the earliest and largest movie palaces constructed in America and is one of the few of its kind extant. The decorative theme was French, not surprising for a city that compared itself to Paris in the Burnham Plan of 1909. The Arc de Triomphe inspired the Chicago Theatre's exterior façade on State Street, the Grand Lobby was modeled after J. H. Mansart's chapel at Versailles, and Louis XIV-style furnishings were placed throughout. Music was provided by the Chicago Theatre Symphony Orchestra and by the famous Chicago Theatre Grande Wurlitzer pipe organ, restored in 1970. Theater design requires an understanding of engineering, acoustics, and interior decoration. Rapp and Rapp became highly successful specialists in this field. Their work includes the Tivoli, Oriental, and Uptown theaters in Chicago, as well as the Times Square and Brooklyn Paramount in New York City.

John Mills Van Osdel
177–91 North State Street
1872

The Page Brothers Building is remarkable for its cast-iron façade, one of two remaining in Chicago's Loop. The former site of the City Hotel, which had been destroyed in the 1871 Chicago fire, this property was developed as a 70-foot-long store and warehouse that was partitioned by brick fire-walls into three separate sections for different tenants. The wholesale leather firm of Page Brothers & Company occupied the corner section. The Page Brothers Building was designed by John Mills Van Osdel, who came to Chicago in 1837 to supervise the building of Mayor William B. Ogden's residence. In 1844, he established Chicago's first architectural practice, which provided many noteworthy structures for the booming young city—grain elevators, the first City Hall, and an elegant Palmer House Hotel. Van Osdel was also responsible for introducing cast-iron architecture to Chicago prior to the Civil War. For this building, he ordered the façade from Daniel D. Badger's Architectural Iron Works in New York. Since the strength of cast iron allowed a greater proportion of glass to solid wall, more natural light was available for interior working or selling space. Further, cast iron's plasticity allowed it to be cast into a variety of ornamental shapes, providing stylish exteriors for competitive enterprises.

Tigerman Fugman McCurry
60 East Lake Street
1984–6

Clever and functional, the façade of this twelve-story parking garage is designed to look like the front of an automobile. The first two stories are retail and office space, with a SelfPark "license plate" in the middle marking the mezzanine level. The parking garage itself is indicated by a center metal grille with turquoise baked-enamel panels from a 1957 Chevrolet color chart. Awnings painted to look like tire treads flank the entrance; above them, near the top of the building, are two acrylic skylights placed to resemble car headlights. The composition is crowned by a draped, helmeted figure resembling a hood ornament. Is he shaking his fist at the world around him or proclaiming the triumph of good design? Perhaps only architect Stanley Tigerman (b. 1930) knows. Born in Chicago, he was trained at the Massachusetts Institute of Technology and the Yale School of Architecture and was Dean of the School of Architecture at the University of Illinois at Chicago before forming Archeworks, a new design school in Chicago. Tigerman's early designs were influenced primarily by the work of Mies van der Rohe, and his career reflects a continuing exploration of modern American values, sometimes with an engaging sense of humor.

27 Marshall Field and Company Store

D. H. Burnham and Co.; Graham, Burnham and Company
Block bounded by Wabash, Washington, State, and Randolph Streets
1892, 1902, 1906, 1907, 1914
Now known as Macy's

"Meet me under the clock," Chicagoans say, and they mean, of course, at Macy's, formerly the Marshall Field and Company store. As the flagship operations of Chicago's legendary retailer, this store was synonymous with State Street shopping. Its oldest section, at Wabash and Washington Streets, resembles an Italian Renaissance palazzo and was completed a year before the World's Columbian Exposition of 1893. However, the main sections of the store, on State Street, completed between 1902 and 1907, reflect the influence of the Beaux Arts classicism featured at the 1893 Fair. The façade is divided into a three-story base, a mid-section of Ionic columns placed between Chicago-style windows, and a classically detailed entablature. The main entrance is marked by four three-story-high columns, emphasizing the building's dignity and formality. The interior has two multi-story atria. At the north end, colorful Louis Comfort Tiffany mosaics face the dome; to the south, classical decorative elements are used with a restrained palette. This design became a prototype for department stores in the United States and abroad. Among the firm's notable retail commissions were Selfridge's (1906) in London, Wanamaker's (1903) and Gimbel's (1909) in New York, and Filene's (1912) in Boston.

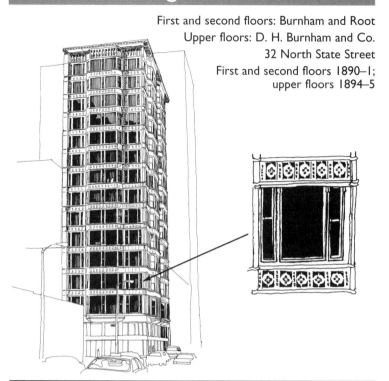

First and second floors: Burnham and Root
Upper floors: D. H. Burnham and Co.
32 North State Street
First and second floors 1890–1;
upper floors 1894–5

The Reliance Building is considered the ultimate skeleton-frame-and-glass representative of the Chicago School of Architecture. At the time of its construction, its Chicago windows were the largest yet built, relative to the building's frame, which itself is thin and light. Only the gothically decorated white terra cotta tiles connect it to an older tradition. The Reliance Building is also notable for its colorful construction history. The site was acquired in 1882 by William Ellery Hale, a prosperous hydraulic elevator manufacturer and friend to Daniel Burnham. Unfortunately his new property could not be redeveloped immediately since it was encumbered by leases expiring at different dates: the lease on the lower two floors expired in May 1890, but the lease on the upper three lasted until 1894. How to maximize investment? John Root's solution was to demolish and reconstruct the lower floors, while supporting the rest of the existing building on huge jacks. The lower floors were then leased to Carson Pirie Scott and Company, while the upper-floor tenants climbed stairs to go about their business. When the leases on the upper floors expired, those floors were replaced with this extraordinary tower by Charles Atwood, who had become Burnham's chief designer after Root's death in 1891.

Louis H. Sullivan
I South State Street
1899, 1903–4
Five bays on State Street: D. H. Burnham and Co., 1906
Three bays on State Street: Holabird and Root, 1960–1
Renovation of rotunda and exterior ornament: John Vinci Associates, 1979
Formerly the Schlesinger and Mayer Store
Now known as the Sullivan Center

Brilliant, visionary, idiosyncratic architect Louis Sullivan (1856–1924) designed this department store at the height of his creative powers. Originally, it was only nine stories high and three bays wide, fronting on Madison Street. Four years later, Sullivan took full advantage of the opportunity to expand the store, now owned by Carson Pirie Scott and Company, to twelve stories that wrap around the crucial corner to State Street, Chicago's retail center. Inside, the spatial organization is functional, efficient, and filled with light. On the exterior, a restrained façade is wedded to extraordinary street-level ornament. Sullivan organized the building in three parts: a simple cornice at top; a midsection, faced in white terra cotta and set with wide Chicago windows, that reveals the underlying structure; and a two-story base with dark, intricate cast-iron ornament that contrasts with the pale façade. In the cartouches framing the doors and display windows, Sullivan gave expression to his theory of natural forms; densely intertwined wreaths create a distinctive entrance that became emblematic of the store in many advertisements. Look for Sullivan's initials, LHS, superimposed on each other at the base of the arches over the State and Madison entrance doors.

Holabird and Roche
7 West Madison Street
1903–4

The fifteen-story Chicago Building, with its dark brown terra cotta façade, is a Chicago School of Architecture gem, displaying all the elements central to the style. The building is divided into a base, thirteen-story shaft, and still intact cornice; its façade expresses the underlying steel frame. Further, it uses two kinds of windows characteristic to Chicago: the projecting bay along narrow Madison Street, which catches available light from three sides, and on wide State Street the flat expanse of a fixed pane flanked on both sides by movable sash windows. Like Holabird and Roche's earlier Marquette Building (see #34), corners are reinforced to emphasize the edge of the block. Construction of the Chicago Building was financed through the creation of the Chicago Savings Bank, which was located in the building until 1913. William Holabird (1854–1923) and Martin Roche (1853–1927) met in the offices of engineer William Le Baron Jenney. Holabird and Roche established their firm in 1883, and it soon became one of Chicago's most successful practices, noted for its clarity of organization and original solutions to tall office building design. Today that tradition is continued by the successor firm Holabird and Root.

Skidmore, Owings & Merrill
30 West Monroe Street
1954–8

The gleaming nineteen-story Inland Steel building was the first commercial office tower to rise in the Loop after the Great Depression and World War II, and the first downtown Chicago project for Skidmore, Owings & Merrill, founded in 1936. Walter Netsch (1920–2008) did the initial design work for the building in 1954; when Netsch took on another assignment, Bruce Graham assumed the project. It was Graham's first major commission, and marks the beginning of a distinguished career that includes the John Hancock Center (1970), Sears Tower (see #14), and One Magnificent Mile (1983). Inland Steel was the prototype of many structural features and commercial amenities that are now commonplace. It was, for instance, the first major building erected on steel pilings rather than concrete caissons; it has a basement parking garage and central air-conditioning. The seven columns located on both its west (Dearborn) and east faces are the building's most striking feature: connected by 60-foot girders, these columns support the entire weight of the building and provide clear-span interior spaces. A separate 25-story service tower to the east, also clad in stainless steel, contains elevators, mechanical systems, and other core facilities, giving the offices maximum layout flexibility.

C. F. Murphy Associates, with The Perkins and Will Partnership
Madison Street between Dearborn and Clark Streets
1964–9
Now known as JPMorgan Chase

The dramatic, graceful inward curve of this 60-story monochromatic buff granite building is functional as well as aesthetic. Since banking public facilities require ample space, they were placed in the building's broad base. Above this two-story lobby, conventional offices house bank employees and other tenants. Elevators are placed at the building's ends to create open floor plans. The rooftop houses a parade of penthouses containing mechanical systems that form a distinctive denticulated silhouette. In 1972, D. H. Burnham and Co.'s 1896 First National Bank Building at the corner of Monroe and Dearborn was demolished to create a sunken plaza from Dearborn to Clark Streets along Monroe Street. This popular plaza is one of three created between Dearborn and Clark Streets during the 1960s to relieve the density of the Loop: to the north is Richard J. Daley Center (see #23) and to the south is Mies van der Rohe's Federal Center (see #35). Note Marc Chagall's mosaic, *The Four Seasons*, the artist's gift to the city of Chicago. Fourteen feet high, ten feet wide, and seventy feet in length, it depicts imagined Chicago scenes.

C. F. Murphy Associates
55 West Monroe
1977–80
Now known as 55 West Monroe

Stretched like a striped silver skin around the corner of Dearborn and Monroe, the 40-story, 800,000-square-foot Xerox Centre is a shining, elegant high-rise in the heart of the Loop. Clad in white-painted aluminum and reflective glass, the walls seem to weave behind the corner tower piece, an illusion created by the different horizontal window levels and the swept-back roof banding. At the street level, diagonal sidewalk paving creates a pattern; on the rooftop, angled striping, visible from taller skyscrapers, repeats this design device. Jahn was born in Germany and received his early training there. At the age of 26, he came to Chicago to study at the Illinois Institute of Technology, where Mies van der Rohe had taught the principles of modern architecture for many years. Historians suggest that Jahn was inspired by Louis Sullivan's Carson Pirie Scott and Company department store (see #29) a block away or by Expressionist Erich Mendelsohn's Schocken Store (1928) in Germany. Whatever the influences, Jahn has a technical virtuosity all his own, integrating historic references into expressive forms and materials with confidence, energy, and power.

Holabird and Roche
140 South Dearborn Street
1893–5
Renovation: Holabird and Root
1979–81

The Marquette Building is a masterpiece of early commercial high-rise architecture. Its exterior grid expresses the underlying skeleton frame, while its wide, flat windows, framed at each side by movable sash, are an early example of the "Chicago window." Yet there is subtlety in this apparent simplicity. The tripartite façade is composed of a two-story base with classically derived terra cotta ornament, such as meander and acanthus leaves; a powerful twelve-story midsection where vertical piers rise smoothly to the roofline and spandrels are recessed; and a two-story decorative cornice, restored in 2003. Corner bays are slightly enlarged and emphasized by horizontal coursing. Owen Aldis, Chicago agent for Boston developers Peter and Shephard Brooks, translated Marquette's journal; his interest in the Northwest Territory's exploration is evident in the decoration of this building, named in Marquette's honor. Bronze bas-reliefs depicting scenes from the life of Marquette enliven the Dearborn Street entrance; a balcony frieze in the rotunda portrays the discovery of the Northwest in mother-of-pearl and favrile-glass panels designed by J. A. Holzer of Tiffany Glass; and Edward Kemeys' bronze heads of Indians and French explorers top the sixteen elevator doors.

Ludwig Mies van der Rohe with Schmidt, Garden, and Erikson;
C. F. Murphy Associates; and A. Epstein and Sons
Dearborn Street between Jackson Boulevard and Adams Street
1959–75

The Federal Center gave Mies van der Rohe (1886–1969) the opportunity
to plan a modern complex in Chicago's Loop amid such Chicago School
masterpieces as the Monadnock and Marquette Buildings (see #6 and
#34). The three government buildings that comprise the Federal Center
all face a large plaza dominated by *Flamingo*, a red metal stabile created by
noted sculptor Alexander Calder (1898–1976). The buildings share common lobby heights, glass and steel exteriors, and light-gray granite floors.
The 30-story Everett McKinley Dirksen Building (1964), a federal courthouse and office building, was the first completed. It stands east of the
plaza, at 230 South Dearborn Street. After Mies died in 1969, architects
Gene Summers (1923–2011) and Bruno Conterato (1920–95) completed
the remaining two buildings of the project: the single-story Post Office
at the southwest corner of Clark and Adams and the 43-story John C.
Kluczynski Office Tower (both 1975). This complex replaced Henry Ives
Cobb's (1859–1931) full-block, classical Federal Building (1905). In 1991,
a fourth federal structure, the Metcalfe Building, was completed at 77
West Jackson Boulevard. Designed by Mies's successor firm, Fujikawa
Johnson and Associates, its form and exterior are consistent with the
existing complex.

Palmer Building: C. M. Palmer
Stone Building: unknown
15–27 West Adams Street
1872 (both)
Formerly known as the Stone and Palmer Buildings

These extraordinary remnants of Chicago history were built immediately after the devastating 1871 fire, in what was then the fringe of the commercial district. They are typical of pre- as well as post-fire construction. Although both buildings were designed in the Italianate style, with rows of arched windows and symmetrical façades, each has unique features. The three-story Stone Building, clad in Cleveland sandstone, is divided into three sections marked by piers articulating the fire wall behind the façade. The center bifora window, a double-arched opening within a larger arched frame, is the building's dominant feature. Incised lines on the exterior provide illusionary joints between regular courses of ashlar-faced rusticated blocks and reinforce the building's surface regularity. The Stone Building's third story was a public meeting hall, the last surviving downtown example of a once common building usage. To the west, the four-story Palmer Building was developed by real estate tycoon Potter Palmer (1826–1902) as part of his extensive property holdings in the Loop. It is one of only two remaining cast-iron-front buildings in Chicago (see #25). Such fashionable façades were prefabricated, bolted together on site, and fastened into the load-bearing masonry walls.

Holabird and Roche
542 South Dearborn Street
1889–91
Renovation: Booth/Hansen & Associates
1985

Named for the great Ottawa Indian chief, Pontiac, who led the 1763–4 uprising against the British in the Great Lakes region, this fourteen-story brick and terra cotta building is located in Printing House Row. It was originally planned for light industrial use. However, by completion of construction, the real estate market had changed, so it was leased for office space instead. One of the first skeleton-frame buildings, its façade is notable for the broad expanses of glass and the projecting bays that capture as much light and air as possible in what was a sooty, noisy section of the city. The two lower stories, still unaltered, are tied together by thin, limestone-clad piers with elegant ornamental capitals. Above them are the richly detailed terra cotta soffits of the bay windows. The Pontiac Building's cornice is still intact, as are many of its interior doors and hardware. The oldest surviving example of Holabird and Roche's work, this building reflects the interplay between solid and void made possible by the skeleton frame and more fully exploited in their later work, including the Monadnock and Marquette Buildings (see #6 and #34).

George C. Nimmons
720–36 South Dearborn Street
1912

This straightforward, thirteen-story red brick loft building was constructed with heavy timbers and reinforced concrete floors to support heavy printing presses and other machinery. Located on Printing House Row, it is distinguished by the polychrome terra cotta panels on its façade, which illustrate the history of printing. Over the entrance a mural depicts the printing of the first book with movable type, the Gutenberg Bible. Spandrels contain geometric patterns, and the terra cotta decoration continues to the top of the building, where a sunburst motif lies at the center of the roofline gable. The façade is composed of a base with nine two-story tapering piers outlined with white terra cotta; a shaft of nine unornamented piers rising from the second to the ninth floors; and a two-story upper section that repeats the tapering piers design. George C. Nimmons (1865–1947) was associated with the Prairie School of architecture that flourished from the turn of the century until World War I. Best known for his commercial work, Nimmons also designed the Reid, Murdoch and Company headquarters on the Chicago River (1913–4) and, in partnership with William K. Fellows, the Sears, Roebuck and Company headquarters complex (1904) on West Arthington Street at Homan Avenue.

Cyrus W. Eidlitz
47 West Polk Street, at the foot of Dearborn Street
1883–5
Formerly the Chicago and Western
Indiana Railway Station

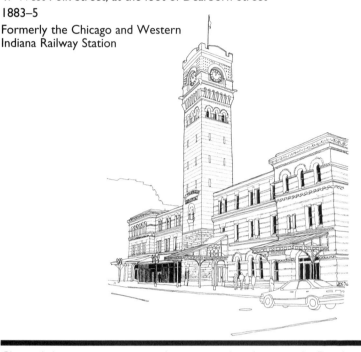

Chicago's last surviving nineteenth-century railroad station, the Dearborn Street Station was developed by a consortium of five railroad companies, headed by the Chicago and Western Indiana line, to secure entry into the city of Chicago. The new station was ensured a prominent site at the foot of Dearborn Street when the city extended the street southward from Van Buren to Polk Street in 1881. Designed by New York architect Cyrus Eidlitz (1858–1923), the Romanesque revival building has a base of pink rusticated granite and walls of red pressed brick with deep red terra cotta details. Originally, the headhouse had gable roofs of vertically striated slate, and the clocktower was capped with a steeply pitched roof as well, but these were destroyed in a 1922 fire. Construction of this important station fostered development of the surrounding land, where the printing industry of the Midwest concentrated around the explosive growth of mail-order catalogs from companies such as Sears Roebuck and Montgomery Ward. After passenger operations ceased in 1971, Dearborn Street Station was renovated as office and retail space and the vast railroad yards behind the station were replaced with small-scale residential development.

Graham, Anderson, Probst and White
210 South Canal Street
1916–25

The Union Station complex combines Beaux Arts grandeur with sophisticated planning, engineering, and railroad technology. It was expected to provide the major link between the Loop, suburban commuting networks, and the planned but never realized Civic Center, which would have been to the west on Congress Street. When completed, it could handle up to 720 trains a day because its double stub-end plan allows trains to move in either direction at either end. The complex was organized as two distinct buildings, the headhouse, or waiting room, and the smaller Concourse Building facing the Chicago River (demolished in 1969); between them was a passageway where ticket offices and baggage facilities were located. From the outside, the waiting room appears as a conventional eight-story office building, but the 100- by 269-foot interior, with its glass skylight vault, grand perimeter Corinthian columns, and Roman travertine walls, is a monumental space, built when people who traveled did so by rail, and terminals had enormous symbolic power. Architect Peirce Anderson (1870–1936) is credited with the design of Union Station. Anderson became Daniel Burnham's chief designer in 1898, after training at Harvard and the Ecole des Beaux-Arts he also designed Union Station in Washington, D.C.

Murphy/Jahn
500 West Madison Street
1979–87

Formerly known as the
Northwestern Atrium

The Ogilvie Transportation Center, which replaced the Beaux Arts masonry Chicago and NorthWestern Terminal designed by Frost and Granger in 1911, is a 37-story, 1.6-million-square-foot glass and aluminum complex. The new building evokes the spatial grandeur of nineteenth-century train stations while dealing with the challenge of multi-use space and levels. Both commuters and tenants enter a 90-foot-high skylit retail gallery that extends the entire length of the façade. Ground-level escalators lead to a 110-foot-high atrium at train level; a second escalator bank leads to the office lobby above. On the exterior, dark-blue enameled aluminum ribbons emphasize the building's verticality; the Art Deco style is suggested by the streamlined horizontal glass curves cascading down the tripartite façade, with its central rounded tower. Note also how the building's Madison Street silhouette echoes that of Riverside Plaza, which was completed in 1929, and how its concentric arched entry recalls those of Chicago's demolished Transportation and Stock Exchange Buildings, both designed by noted architect Louis Sullivan in the late nineteenth century. This complex is a fine example of architect Helmut Jahn's work, which integrates curving, muscular, colorful forms with structural expressiveness.

Perkins & Will
One North Halsted
1998–2002

It can't be missed, this 39-story concrete and glass high-rise that sits on a narrow site between the eight-lane Kennedy Expressway at its feet and the low-rise Greektown/industrial-loft neighborhood to the west. Staking out new territory westward for luxury residential towers, Skybridge marks a dramatic transition in scale between the downtown Loop and the Near West Side. Winner of a competition held among three invited firms, Ralph Johnson (b. 1948) of Perkins & Will designed a porous, asymmetrical composition for this 850,000-square-foot mixed-use skyscraper. The six-story base includes a grocery store, coffee shop, and a parking garage masked by a glass curtain wall. But the real attention-grabber is above this space: Instead of a single slab, the 237-unit residential tower is punctuated by a series of indentations of voids and bridges and balconies that both protrude and recess. Above the 14th floor is a 250-foot void dividing the building into two towers that are crossed by glass bridges. On the north façade, a 4-story opening from the 10th to the 14th floors creates a giant window. At the top, a giant, cantilevered trellis caps the roof, integrating the towers that were separated below. Color is used to highlight notches and setbacks, animating the concrete surface.

John Alexander Low Waddell
El stations: A. M. Hedley, consulting architect
Lake Street to Wabash Avenue to Van Buren Street to Wells Street
1892–1908

The Loop's elevated train is a powerful symbol of the connections between commerce, transportation, land values, politics, and emerging technology that existed in turn-of-the-century Chicago. Explosive economic growth concentrated in Chicago's small business district created very congested streets, so an alternative was sought to the slow, street-running cable cars. (The cable cars' turnabouts along Lake, Wabash, Madison, and State had created the first "loop" in 1882.) John Alexander Low Waddell (1854–1938) designed a two-track railroad running on steel trestle bents with open-webbed trusses or riveted plate girders carried on columns 70 feet apart. It was built between 1892 and 1908 by various independent companies, beginning with the Chicago and South Side Rapid Transit Railroad, which created its first line in 1892 to transport passengers to the World's Columbian Exposition of 1893. This was followed by the Lake Street line (1893); the Metropolitan West Side Elevated Railroad (1895), which was the first electrically powered line; and the Union Elevated Railway (1897), built by entrepreneur Charles T. Yerkes to connect these lines in a loop. In 1900, the Northwestern Elevated (Ravenswood line) was added. In 1924, these lines were consolidated as the Chicago Rapid Transit Company.

The Riverfront

The Riverfront

NORTH KINGSBURY

CHICAGO RIVER

17

16

N LARRABEE ST

W CHICAGO AVE

WEST ERIE

WEST ONTARIO

WEST OHIO

GRAND

ILLINOIS

HUBBARD

KINZIE

15 14

18

19

12 11 10

13

CHICAGO RIVER

32 33 34 WACKER 35 36

31

30

LAKE

20

RANDOLPH

WASHINGTON

22 21 29

MADISON

28

MONROE

CLINTON CANAL 23 WACKER FRANKLIN WELLS LASALLE CLARK DEARBORN STATE

ADAMS

27 26

JACKSON

25

VAN BUREN

CONGRESS PKWY.

HARRISON

POLK

24

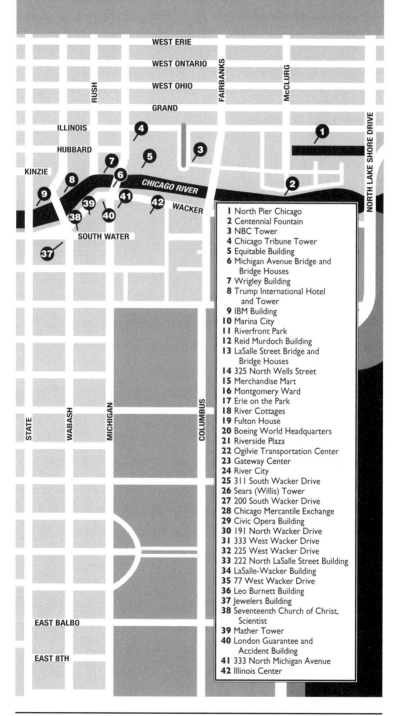

WEST ERIE

WEST ONTARIO

WEST OHIO

GRAND

ILLINOIS

HUBBARD

KINZIE

RUSH

FAIRBANKS

McCLURG

NORTH LAKE SHORE DRIVE

CHICAGO RIVER

WACKER

SOUTH WATER

STATE

WABASH

MICHIGAN

COLUMBUS

EAST BALBO

EAST 8TH

1 North Pier Chicago
2 Centennial Fountain
3 NBC Tower
4 Chicago Tribune Tower
5 Equitable Building
6 Michigan Avenue Bridge and Bridge Houses
7 Wrigley Building
8 Trump International Hotel and Tower
9 IBM Building
10 Marina City
11 Riverfront Park
12 Reid Murdoch Building
13 LaSalle Street Bridge and Bridge Houses
14 325 North Wells Street
15 Merchandise Mart
16 Montgomery Ward
17 Erie on the Park
18 River Cottages
19 Fulton House
20 Boeing World Headquarters
21 Riverside Plaza
22 Ogilvie Transportation Center
23 Gateway Center
24 River City
25 311 South Wacker Drive
26 Sears (Willis) Tower
27 200 South Wacker Drive
28 Chicago Mercantile Exchange
29 Civic Opera Building
30 191 North Wacker Drive
31 333 West Wacker Drive
32 225 West Wacker Drive
33 222 North LaSalle Street Building
34 LaSalle-Wacker Building
35 77 West Wacker Drive
36 Leo Burnett Building
37 Jewelers Building
38 Seventeenth Church of Christ, Scientist
39 Mather Tower
40 London Guarantee and Accident Building
41 333 North Michigan Avenue
42 Illinois Center

Christian A. Eckstorm

Cityfront Center adjacent to Ogden Slip, 435 East Illinois Street

1905–20

Adaptive reuse: Booth/Hansen & Associates, 1986–8

Formerly Pugh Warehouse

Work on the Pugh Warehouse, named for developer James Andrew Pugh and designed by Christian Albert Eckstorm, began in 1905. Sections were gradually added, until by 1920 it stretched 1,663 feet eastward to the shore of Lake Michigan. Originally, it was the home of numerous manufacturers who displayed their products for the wholesale market. Later, after the larger Merchandise and Furniture Marts were built in the 1920s, it became a storage warehouse. Its location on protected Ogden Slip adjacent to the Chicago River and the lakefront allowed merchandise to be shipped easily by boat or by the rail lines that extended to the slip from the west. North Pier was part of an area of low-rise warehouses that stored lumber, grain, paper, and candy products. Today, this historic brick structure has been imaginatively adapted to new uses as a retail, office, dining, and recreational center To create greater accessibility and better views, architect Laurence Booth (b. 1936) designed two three-story glass galleries along the waterside. Their simple, rectangular lines recall the functional form of the warehouse itself.

Lohan Associates
Cityfront Center at the McClurg Court Esplanade
1989

The Centennial Fountain commemorates the founding of the Metropolitan Water Reclamation District in 1889, the authority that was responsible for reversing the course of the Chicago River and today manages Chicago area water treatment. Before 1900, the Chicago River carried waste directly to Lake Michigan, the source of the city's drinking water. Periodic cholera epidemics threatened the population's health until the Sanitary and Ship Canal (1892–1900) was completed. Since the new canal bed was lower than that of the Chicago River, simple gravity diverted the river flow into the canal and away from the lake. Architect Dirk Lohan's (b. 1938) fountain design mirrors the divided flow of the water at the mouth of the river. The eastern half of the fountain symbolizes the river's connection to Lake Michigan and through the Great Lakes to the Atlantic Ocean, while the western half represents the river's flow to the Des Plaines and Mississippi Rivers, then into the Gulf of Mexico. From the fountain's collecting pool, the water funnels into a cannon that projects a dramatic 80-foot-high water arch across the 222-foot-wide Chicago River to the opposite bank.

Skidmore, Owings & Merrill
200 East Illinois Street
1985–9

Architect Adrian Smith's (b. 1944) NBC Tower was the first new building completed in Cityfront Center, the 60-acre multi-use development bordered by the Chicago River to the south. NBC Tower not only meets the guidelines set forth by Cityfront Center's Master Plan for materials and scale but also gracefully evokes the past. For example, NBC's soaring verticality, sleek setbacks, and masonry exterior recall the 333 North Michigan Avenue building across the river, while its load-bearing buttresses reference those of the nearby Tribune Tower (see #4). Here, the façade is articulated by rough-cut limestone piers alternating with coated precast spandrels finished to resemble terra cotta. The east and west entrances are detailed with intricate bronze metalwork and are further emphasized by a central bowed window that extends the entire height of the building and culminates in a spire facing Michigan Avenue. An adjacent four-story broadcasting studio continues the rhythm of the tower base elements and is connected to the tower by an interior lobby. This sensitive handling of form, materials, and site results in a romantic addition to the Chicago skyline.

Tower, Hood and Howells; printing plant, Jarvis Hunt (1859–1941)
435 North Michigan Avenue
Tower, 1922–5; printing plant, 1916–20

In 1922, the Chicago Tribune announced what became one of the twentieth century's most famous architectural competitions: $100,000 in prize money to design its new headquarters on a site near the just-completed Michigan Avenue Bridge and adjacent to the Tribune's new printing plant on the Chicago River, where the waterway facilitated shipment of newsprint and other operations. The 264 competition entries from around the world included a fascinating range of designs for "the world's most beautiful office building." The winning entry, by Raymond Hood and John Mead Howells of New York, dresses a plain limestone shaft with the gargoyle gutters and flamboyant flying buttresses of France's great Gothic cathedrals. The grand arched entry and surrounding allegorical figures are impressive, but the tower steals the scene: a crown of open tracery that remains as visible and photogenic today as it was in 1922. Ironically, the contest's most influential entry may not have been the winner, but Finnish architect Eliel Saarinen's second-place design. Its strongly rooted and elegantly set-back mass helped define the skyscraper form for the rest of the century. Hood himself referred to it in his later designs in New York for the Daily News Building and Rockefeller Center complex.

Skidmore, Owings & Merrill
401 North Michigan Avenue
1962–5

On this site, pioneer Jean Baptiste du Sable, Chicago's first permanent settler, built his cabin. Now a 35-story office tower of glazed bronze solar glass with an aluminum curtain wall rises, recalling the structurally expressive style of noted architect Ludwig Mies van der Rohe (1886–1969). This aesthetic was often used by Skidmore, Owings & Merrill in its commercial high-rise designs. Here design partner Bruce Graham (1925–2010) used granite spandrels to mark the floors, while slender vertical piers containing circular pipes divide the windows into sets of four. This pattern gives the façade a subtle rhythm, enhanced when the Chicago River is reflected in the glass. The Chicago Tribune sold the land to the Equitable Life Assurance Society on condition that the new structure be no taller than the Tribune Tower and that, set back from Michigan Avenue, it not obstruct the Tribune's views. Pioneer Court, a plaza connecting the two buildings, is often used for summertime art exhibitions; via a sweeping spiral staircase, it also provides public access to the riverbank below. Such access was an amenity envisioned in the 1909 Plan of Chicago by architects Daniel Burnham and Edward Bennett.

Michigan Avenue Bridge and Bridge Houses 6

Edward H. Bennett, architect; Thomas Pihlfeldt, engineer of bridges;
Hugh Young, engineer of bridge design; Henry Herring and J. E. Fraser,
sculptors
Michigan Avenue and the Chicago River
1918–20; Pylon sculptures,1928

The Michigan Avenue Bridge blended the Beaux Arts aesthetics of Daniel
Burnham's 1909 Plan of Chicago with the sophisticated engineering
necessary to solve one of Chicago's worst transportation problems.
Before 1920, when Michigan Avenue still ended at the river, nearly
half of Chicago's north-south traffic converged at the old Rush Street
swing bridge, which was also among the first bridges encountered by
ships entering from the lake. To ease the resulting congestion, Chicago
engineers perfected a bridge type in which leaves divide, rotate around
a trunnion pin, and return to their fixed positions. The Michigan Avenue
Bridge was their masterpiece: the world's first double-leaf, double-deck
trunnion bascule bridge, capable of handling two levels of traffic and still
clearing the channel in under 60 seconds. Much of Burnham's grand, classical design, modeled after the Seine bridges of Paris, was implemented
after Burnham's death by Edward Bennett (1874–1954), consultant to
the Chicago Plan Commission. Bennett's four limestone bridge houses
create a monumental approach to this important crossing, while commemorative sculptures by J. E. Fraser and Henry Herring mark the historic
location, spanning the sites of Fort Dearborn and Chicago's first pioneer
homesteads.

Wrigley Building

Graham, Anderson, Probst and White
410 North Michigan Avenue
1919–22 (south tower);
1924–5 (north tower)

The Wrigley Building may be Chicago's favorite landmark. Its gleaming white façade and gently curving entrance plaza convey a bright, welcoming feeling; most familiar of all is the eleven-story clocktower, inspired by the Giralda Tower in Seville, Spain, which has also been spotlit at night from the outset. The building was developed by William Wrigley, founder of the chewing gum company, and was, for many years, the Wrigley Company headquarters. As the first building completed north of the Chicago River on the newly extended Michigan Avenue, it initiated the area's redevelopment from a dingy warehouse district to a desirable commercial address. A second building was added to the north in 1925, and is connected to the first at the lobby and by an upper-level skywalk. Both are sheathed in terra cotta, a material popular both for its decorative potential, and for its fireproofing ability, not underestimated in a city leveled by fire just 50 years before. To encourage public access to the Chicago River, a monumental staircase was designed that leads from the entrance plaza to a riverside landing where tour boats dock in the summertime.

Trump International Hotel and Tower 8

Skidmore, Owings & Merrill
401 N. Wabash
2009

Donald Trump's signature Chicago building was bound to be bold, but could it be beautiful as well as just big? At hand were two major assets: master high-rise designer Adrian Smith and a superb site on the Chicago River made available when the low-slung modernist Chicago Sun-Times Building was demolished. Smith designed curved corners and staggered setbacks at floors 16, 29, and 51 to indicate functional changes, help reduce wind forces and provide contextual relationships with shorter landmark neighbors. The first setback marks the transition from the lobby and parking levels to the luxury hotel; the second from the hotel to the condominiums, and the third references the height of Mies van der Rohe's iconic IBM Building nearby. In 2009, this 92-story, 1,388-foot structure became the tallest residential tower in the United States. Set parallel to the Chicago River but entered on Wabash Avenue, Trump Tower connects to the waterway below by a public zigzag landscaped walkway. The façade is sheathed in glass set in an aluminum and mirror-finished stainless steel latticework that refracts and reflects sunlight. Best seen from afar, note how this statuesque skyscraper with the shiny skin, well placed curves, and impressive height claims her place on the skyline.

Ludwig Mies van der Rohe with C. F. Murphy Associates
330 North Wabash Avenue, between Wabash and State on the Chicago River
1969–71

The IBM Building was the last project designed by Mies van der Rohe, one of this century's most influential architects. Born in Germany and named director of the progressive Bauhaus School in 1930, he left the country amid increasing political unrest and, recruited by John Holabird of the Chicago architectural firm Holabird and Root, in 1938 became Director of Architecture at Chicago's Armour (later Illinois) Institute of Technology. Mies believed that the twentieth century required a new architecture using modern materials and simplified forms. The 52-story IBM Building exemplifies characteristics of his best works: harmonious proportions, elegant materials, and the expression of the building's underlying form through steel and glass. Here, the steel frame and ample 30- by 40-foot bay modules are directly expressed on the exterior's curtain wall of aluminum and double-glazed tinted glass. Placement on the narrow K-shaped site had to accommodate existing train tracks and Chicago Sun-Times storage facilities while providing view corridors to Lake Michigan—constraints that restricted public access to the river's edge. Nonetheless, the IBM Building remains a cool, contained punctuation mark to the 1920s decorative designs along Wacker Drive and the Michigan Avenue Bridge.

Bertrand Goldberg Associates
300 North State Street, between State and Dearborn Streets
1964–7

Marina City is noteworthy for its consideration of urban issues as well as for its innovative engineering and design. Commissioned by the International Union of Janitors, architect Bertrand Goldberg (1913–97) sought to provide attractive, affordable housing in downtown Chicago while incorporating the Chicago River, then a neglected resource, into his design. This "city within a city" originally comprised 900 apartment units in two towers, an office building, restaurants, a theater, and recreational facilities for its residents. Goldberg's recognition of the river as an amenity can be seen in the building's marina, which allows residents to take advantage of their riverfront location. When completed in 1967, the reinforced concrete towers were the tallest in the world; their curving shell forms are functional in their reduction of wind shear, and aesthetic in their exploration of the sculptural possibilities of the material. The method of construction was especially inventive. Because a concrete core, where utilities are located, was built first, the concrete floors could then be poured and attached sequentially in a process that was both time- and cost-efficient. Note the repetition of cantilevered apartment balconies, which creates a distinctive scalloped silhouette.

Quaker Tower
Skidmore, Owings & Merrill
321 North Clark Street
1983–7

Hotel Nikko Chicago
Hellmuth, Obata & Kassabaum
320 North Dearborn Street
1985–7
Now known as the
Westin Chicago River North

Part of an ensemble fronting the Chicago River that also includes the adjacent Westin Chicago River North, Quaker Tower is a 35-story metal and glass flat-roofed tower containing one million square feet of office space. Designed by Bruce Graham in association with studio heads Diane Legge Kemp and Richard Tomlinson, Quaker Tower's understated elegance results from the use of blue-green glass to reflect the river's color and a grid of rounded exterior stainless steel mullions that sparkle in the sunlight. A block-long pedestrian promenade connects the tower with the hotel and also provides public access to the river. This walkway is landscaped with continuous rows of upright yews fronted by spreading junipers, creating an inviting, green oasis. A mezzanine level has outdoor seating. At the corner of Clark Street and the river, a small building housing the elevator to the riverwalk mimics the nearby bridge houses, creating a further connection to the riverfront.

Reid Murdoch Building 12

George C. Nimmons
325 North LaSalle Street
1913–4
Also known as the Central Office Building

Built for the Reid, Murdoch, and Company wholesale food operation, this building is one of the last remaining warehouse structures along the main branch of the Chicago River and was adaptively reused for City of Chicago offices in 1955. Reflecting its steel and concrete frame, the red brick exterior is a simple rectangular grid, which is enlivened by dark red terra cotta details, including a lion's head emblematic of the company's Monarch brand name. The riverfront façade balances the horizontality of the building itself with the vertical thrust of a three-story clocktower. The building was once symmetrical; however, one 20-foot bay was removed in 1926 when LaSalle Street was widened in preparation for its new bridge. On the building's north side there were originally 40- by 240-foot freight train sheds for two sets of railroad tracks. On the river side were docking facilities, and the pedestrian promenade still extends along the Chicago River at street level. The building's architect, George Nimmons (1865–1947), was associated with the Prairie School of architecture; in 1904, he and William K. Fellows (1870–1948) co-designed the Sears, Roebuck & Company complex on West Arthington Street at Homan Avenue—at the time, the largest Chicago building commission ever received.

13 LaSalle Street Bridge and Bridge Houses

Edward H. Bennett, architect; Thomas G. Pihlfeldt, engineer of bridges;
Donald N. Becker, engineer of bridge design
LaSalle Street and the Chicago River
1927–8

This trunnion bascule bridge at LaSalle Street, 86 feet wide and 242
feet across, is second only to the Michigan Avenue Bridge in scale and
grandeur. Since the 1909 Plan of Chicago recommended widening LaSalle
Street to better organize downtown traffic circulation, the LaSalle Street
Bridge received monumental treatment. Planning began in 1914–15, but
lack of funding, local protests, and the onset of World War I delayed
construction until 1927. At that time, the southern end of Wacker Drive
had just been completed (1924–6) and the widening of LaSalle Street at
the north end—which resulted in the Central Office Building (see #11)
losing a bay—coincided with the commencement of bridge construction.
Like the adjacent Clark Street Bridge, built one year later, the LaSalle
Street Bridge is supported by pony trusses that provide graceful curved
silhouettes where the bridge meets the riverbank. These low trusses do
not interfere with sightlines and have no overhead bracing. Heavily ornamented bridge houses designed by architect Edward Bennett distinguish
the LaSalle Street Bridge and emphasize its importance. Made of Bedford
limestone, they are taller and more detailed than most, with mansard
roofs, cartouches, swags, and rusticated masonry.

1914

Adaptive reuse:
Booth/Hansen &
Associates, 1985

Formerly the
Chase & Sanborn
Coffee warehouse

This building is a fine example of adaptive reuse; architect Laurence Booth (b. 1936) transformed a small, neglected coffee warehouse into the corporate headquarters for Helene Curtis Industries. On the exterior, the façade was kept intact with the addition of a curved green glass rooftop penthouse, which served as the corporate board room. Its rounded center recalls a ship's prow, an appropriate reference for the Chicago River, once one of the busiest waterways in the world. The proximity of the river eliminates the need for cooling towers on the roof: river water is circulated through coils in the basement as part of the air-conditioning system. The interior space, organized around the 18- by 20-foot column spacing, allowed for the grouping of workstations, while the columns also functioned as monumental light fixtures. At the lower level facing the river, a cafeteria and riverfront terrace offered amenities for employees. Helene Curtis Industries recently moved out of this location and relocated to Michigan Avenue in Chicago. The building currently awaits another opportunity for renewal and use.

Graham, Anderson, Probst and White

Merchandise Mart Plaza, north bank of the Chicago River between Wells and Orleans Streets

1923–31

The massive Merchandise Mart, comprising nearly 4 million square feet, was the largest building in the world until the completion of the Pentagon near Washington, D.C. The Merchandise Mart's five-acre site along the main channel of the Chicago River near the junction of its north and south branches gives it exceptional visual prominence from three directions. The 1909 Plan of Chicago encouraged riverfront development, and Marshall Field and Company decided to consolidate the company's wholesale operations here. Soon space was leased to other distributors as well. Built over the NorthWestern train tracks, the Merchandise Mart is among Chicago's first air rights developments and was expected to be part of a new business district north of the river until the Great Depression intervened. Framed in steel and sheathed in buff Bedford limestone, its large mass is articulated by a series of horizontal cornice lines, a central shaft and tower, corner bays capped with turrets, and green and gold accents. The lobby is decorated with murals by Jules Guerin, who also illustrated the 1909 Plan of Chicago. Enhanced by its recent cleaning and renovation, its site, scale, and stylized details create a powerful presence on the Chicago River.

Warehouse: Schmidt, Garden, and Martin
Merchandise building: Company in-house design staff
Tower: Minoru Yamasaki
618 West Chicago Avenue and the north branch of the Chicago River
Warehouse, 1906–8; merchandise building, 1929; tower, 1974

Snaking along the north branch of the Chicago River, this cream-colored, nine-story trapezoidal mass averaging 800 by 200 feet was the largest reinforced concrete building of its time when it was completed in 1908. It was the second Montgomery Ward Company commission for Richard Schmidt (1865–1958), who had previously designed the company's new office tower (see Michigan Avenue #17). This warehouse complex, which consolidated all company operations, was located along the Chicago River to take advantage of both rail and water transport for the distribution of mail-order goods. It follows the river edge with sleek horizontal lines interspersed with stylized, decorative motifs common to the Prairie School of architecture. This style is known for its use of long, low lines and geometric patterns, suggesting the flat vistas of the midwestern prairie, and can be seen in Frank Lloyd Wright's concurrent work. Schmidt was born in Germany but came to Chicago a year later; he studied architecture at the Massachusetts Institute of Technology. In 1906 Schmidt and fellow architect Hugh Garden (1873–1961) designed the elegant Madlener House, home of the Graham Foundation for Advanced Studies in the Fine Arts. They later formed a successful partnership with architect Edgar Martin (1871–1951).

520 West Erie
Lucien Lagrange Architects
1999–2002

When it opened, Erie on the Park, a 25-story condominium tower, was a surprise. Its raw industrial vocabulary came unexpectedly from architect Lucien Lagrange (b. 1940), best known for designing luxury residences including the 67-story Park Tower or elegant, Parisian-inspired condominiums. Even Lagrange's retail work, Plaza Escada on Michigan Avenue, appeals to the elite. But Lagrange had once worked closely with Bruce Graham and engineer Fazlur Khan, both of whom were responsible for the Sears and John Hancock skyscrapers, known for their powerful steel structural expression. He deftly applies this experience to Erie on the Park, designing a successful project for both the user and the public. How? First, his choice to use steel rather than concrete framing better addressed wind and other stresses on the narrow, 10,000-square-foot parallelogram-shaped site. Steel also required fewer columns, thus offering flexibility to maximize residential layouts, unit heights, and balcony options. Furthermore, while the interior bracing is hidden, the exterior bracing is exposed as 3-story silver chevrons climbing the northeast and southwest sides. They animate the façade and lead the eye upward to the open steel frame at the top. Blue-tinted glass and bands of steel spandrels add more visual panache.

River Cottages 18

Harry Weese and Associates
357–65 North Canal Street
1990

These four River Cottages facing the Chicago River are located at the foot of the Kinzie Street Bridge, the terminus of Chicago's first railroad line, the Galena and Chicago Union. In November 1848, the first grain transported by rail arrived at this site, where it was loaded onto ships for transport to eastern markets. Smaller boats, owned by residents, now moor at the River Cottages. These five- and six-level townhouses have units ranging from 2,200 to 4,200 square feet. An internal elevator and stairs connect the various living levels. The stucco townhouses have tubular steel frames and concrete deck floors. Their articulated cross-bracing and angular profile are reminiscent of the historic schooner sails and riggings familiar to architect Harry Weese (1915–98), an accomplished sailor. Weese, who received his architectural training at the Massachusetts Institute of Technology and Cranbrook Academy, devoted much of his career to the planning, preservation, and improvement of the Chicago riverfront. In this imaginative design, portholes, decks, and balconies all reference the river. Such small-scale development is rare along valuable waterfront property and makes a special contribution to the cityscape.

Fulton House

Frank Abbott
345 North Canal Street
1908
Adaptive reuse: Harry Weese and Associates, 1979–81
Formerly American Cold
Storage Warehouse

Standing between the train tracks and the Chicago River, the sixteen-story pink brick American Cold Storage Warehouse was among Chicago's first steel and concrete buildings. Architect Harry Weese faced several problems when he began to renovate the structure in 1979 for residential condominium use. First of all, the original building had been constructed in two phases, each with its own structural system—one of poured-in-place reinforced concrete spanning steel beams, the other with vaulted light-weight aggregate floors. Weese rebuilt these sections where necessary to form an integrated frame. Next, the architect had to create 500 windows for the planned living units, which required punching through exterior masonry walls 12 to 16 inches thick without damaging their structural integrity. He met this challenge by devising a system that allowed the walls to be cut through from both sides. This adaptive reuse project, success-fully completed in 1981, created 104 loft-style condominiums, including top floor duplexes, and 20,000 square feet of commercial space at the building's base. Renamed Fulton House, it provides superb views and accessibility to Chicago's Loop, while offering residents boat moorings and a waterside deck.

Perkins & Will

100 North Riverside Plaza, between Randolph and Washington Streets

1988–90

Formerly known as the Morton International Building

This 36-story, mixed-use skyscraper presented several challenges to architect Ralph Johnson (b. 1948) and his project team. It was a particularly difficult site—long, narrow, irregular, and bounded by the Chicago River on the east. Furthermore, the passage through this site by the busy Metra commuter railroad line added the complication of building over existing tracks and rights-of-way. Johnson's design differentiates the various building uses as simple rectilinear blocks with geometric patterns on the gray granite, glass, and metal exterior. These blocks are then connected by a pedestrian arcade of 15-foot repeating columns and by a clocktower placed asymmetrically toward the northern end of the building. This clocktower is a public amenity in itself and recalls others along the riverfront at the Central Office Building (see #12) and the Wrigley Building (see #7). Since a structural column could not be placed where the train tracks curved, a rooftop truss was used to redistribute loads. This exposed form reflects the structure of nearby Chicago River bridges. In order to ensure public access to the riverfront, a linear park at the river's edge was retained, with stairways leading to it from the street level.

Holabird and Root
400 West Madison Street
1925–9
Formerly the Chicago Daily News Building

Headquarters for the old Chicago Daily News during its heyday, this was the first building in Chicago to use the air rights above railroad tracks and it pioneered development across the Chicago River west of the Loop. Initial framing problems were solved by using large double 12-foot girders to cantilever parts of the building over the tracks. Placed parallel to the Chicago River at the western edge of its block-long site, the 26-story limestone building is intersected by a series of piers at its base that are repeated on a grander scale at the edges and sides of the building. Its flat central slab is punctuated by slightly recessed rectangular windows. Alvin Meyer's bas-reliefs depict the history of printing at ground level and a two-story covered concourse connects Riverside Plaza to the Ogilvie Transportation Center (see #22). The plaza's pedestrian walkway along the river was the site of nightly band concerts in the 1930s. A fine example of the 1920s style called Art Moderne (or Art Deco when highly decorated), the building's bold design and innovative engineering won gold medals in 1930 from both the Architectural League of New York and the American Institute of Architects.

Murphy/Jahn
500 West Madison Street
1979–87
Formerly known as the
Northwestern Atrium

The Ogilvie Transportation Center, which replaced the Beaux Arts masonry Chicago and NorthWestern Terminal designed by Frost and Granger in 1911, is a 37-story, 1.6-million-square-foot glass and aluminum complex. The new building evokes the spatial grandeur of nineteenth-century train stations while dealing with the challenge of multi-use space and levels. Both commuters and tenants enter a 90-foot-high skylit retail gallery that extends the entire length of the façade. Ground-level escalators lead to a 110-foot-high atrium at train level; a second escalator bank leads to the office lobby above. On the exterior, dark-blue enameled aluminum ribbons emphasize the building's verticality; the Art Deco style is suggested by the streamlined horizontal glass curves cascading down the tripartite façade, with its central rounded tower. Note also how the building's Madison Street silhouette echoes that of Riverside Plaza, which was completed in 1929, and how its concentric arched entry recalls those of Chicago's demolished Transportation and Stock Exchange Buildings, both designed by noted architect Louis Sullivan in the late nineteenth century. This complex is a fine example of architect Helmut Jahn's work, which integrates curving, muscular, colorful forms with structural expressiveness.

Gateway I–IV and MidAmerica Commodity Exchange
Skidmore, Owings & Merrill
100–300 South Riverside Plaza
1963–83

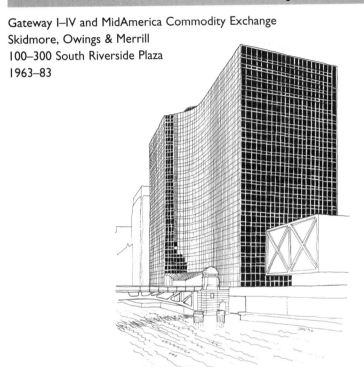

Gateway Center is a five-building project built along the west bank of the Chicago River over railroad tracks that lead to Union Station. All of the Gateway Center buildings except Gateway IV were designed by Bruce Graham. Gateways I and II are identical twenty-story glass and black steel office towers that echo the historic twin brick Butler Brothers Warehouses along the Chicago River to the north, built by the successor offices of Daniel Burnham in 1913 and 1922. Gateway III is a 35-story steel frame office building. Next to it is the five-story MidAmerica Commodity Exchange, marked by exposed X-braces and cantilevered over the commuter entrance to Union Station. In the mid-1980s, the pedestrian plaza along the Chicago River connecting these buildings was improved with additional landscaping and public amenities. Gateway IV, the last and largest building of the group, was designed by James DeStefano (b. 1938). Its 22 stories contain over one million square feet of office space. The curving façade of reflective glass complements a bend in the Chicago River and contrasts with the rigid rectangles of the other four Gateway Center buildings. Note the commuter train activity visible at the lower level.

Bertrand Goldberg Associates
800 South Wells Street
Phase I 1984–6

The serpentine concrete curves of River City hug the Chicago River just south of the Loop. This complex, ten to seventeen stories high, contains 446 apartments, retail and commercial space and a health club. Built on land previously owned by the Baltimore and Ohio Railroad, the project was originally intended to be four 85-story towers linked by skywalks, but the City of Chicago approved a lower scale and density for the site. River City expresses architect Bertrand Goldberg's continuing interest in designing urban complexes that combine affordable housing with working and recreational amenities, as evidenced in his earlier Marina City project (see #10). A native of Chicago, Goldberg trained at Harvard University and at the Bauhaus in Germany under Mies van der Rohe. Other well-known Chicago buildings by Goldberg include the Raymond Hilliard Center (1966) and Northwestern University's Prentice Women's Hospital and Maternity Center (1975), now demolished. His work is informed by his commitment to using architecture to help solve urban issues, his use of concrete as an expressive sculptural material, and his pioneering regard for the Chicago riverfront.

Kohn Pedersen Fox
Associate Architects: Harwood K. Smith
and Partners
1990

Standing in the shadow of the legendary Willis (formerly Sears) Tower,
this 65-story, 1.4-million-square-foot building was the tallest reinforced
concrete structure in the world when it was completed in 1990. One of
three towers planned for this block-long site facing South Wacker Drive,
311 South Wacker Drive is distinguished by red/pink granite cladding and,
at night, by the brightly lit glass cylinder crowning its tower. The building
is centered around a "winter garden," a glass vaulted area intended to act
as a hub for the complex that includes giant palm trees, a waterfall, and
a restaurant. The massing of the building explores a variety of geometric
configurations: the octagonal tower above the fifty-first floor rises from
a rectangular midsection that in turn is grounded in an irregularly shaped
base. To bind together the elements of the design, architect William
Pedersen (b. 1938) repeated the horizontal banding at the base of the
thirteenth and forty-sixth floors. Pedersen's firm, Kohn Pedersen Fox,
founded in 1976 in New York City, has designed several large buildings
in Chicago (see #30, #31, #32, and Michigan Avenue #51).

Skidmore, Owings & Merrill
233 South Wacker Drive
1968–74; entrance addition, 1984–5
Renovation: DeStefano + Partners, 1992–3
Now known as the Willis Tower

At 110 stories and 1,454 feet high, the Willis Tower is among the tallest buildings in the world. To ensure stability, a system of 75-foot-square structural tubes is used to act as perimeter columns, bracing the skyscraper against powerful wind forces. Nine of these huge tubes form the building's base. As the building rises, the number of tubes is reduced where setbacks occur: at the fiftieth, sixty-sixth, and ninetieth floors. Two tubes remain to support the tower, while steel columns comprising the building's frame serve to channel wind shear and gravity stress down to bedrock caissons. Design partner Bruce Graham (b. 1925–2010) and engineer Fazlur Khan (1929–82) led the project team for this immense undertaking. It both symbolized Sears, Roebuck and Company's position as the largest retailer in the world and consolidated the company's offices. With its dark angular silhouette, the Sears Tower soon became a Chicago icon, but it was forbidding at street level. Several years ago, Skidmore, Owings & Merrill returned to design a vaulted atrium as a friendlier entrance and to renovate the lobby. Recent work by DeStefano + Partners has created a more inviting lobby and better tourist access.

Harry Weese and Associates
1979–81

This 38-story, 850,000-square-foot office tower is situated on a small, irregular site, yet architect Harry Weese's design maximizes both floor size and riverside location. Weese's fascination with the triangular form, seen in other Chicago works, such as the Swiss Grand Hotel in Illinois Center (see #42) and the River Cottages (see #18), is also evident here: the asymmetrical four-sided polygon is composed of two right triangles sharing a hypotenuse. The triangles' differing heights—one rises seven stories above the other—reveal the geometric configuration. A special feature of the building is its three-story glass-enclosed lobby facing the Chicago River that fills the interior with natural light. This emphasis on light is also evident in the building's exterior: white painted aluminum panels alternating with reflective glass give the building a bright sparkling façade among its darker high-rise neighbos. In 1988, Harry Weese designed Quincy Park, adjacent to the tower at the river's edge. This pocket park was donated by developers John Buck, Wes Irvine, and JMB/Urban and modeled on Manhattan's Paley Park. The park's summertime seating, greenery, and waterfall make it a special riverfront amenity.

Fujikawa Johnson and Associates
10 and 30 South Wacker Drive
1983–7

This carnelian granite complex comprises two 1.1-million-square-foot office towers flanking the ten-story Chicago Mercantile Exchange. Beneath its smooth exterior and simple massing are sophisticated solutions to several engineering and design challenges. Since the Exchange required a 40,000-square-foot space with no supporting columns to provide maximum visibility for trading activity, engineers used 140- by 35-foot trusses to support the ceiling, then redistributed this weight to a thickened wall system and wide perimeter columns. These walls would have caused the towers to tilt under their own weight, so the towers were built slightly bowed; as they were occupied, the curves corrected themselves until the towers became properly aligned. Since the site measured 17,000 square feet less than the building program requirements, additional leasing space was provided by cantilevering both towers 32 feet over the Mercantile Exchange. Finally, financial prudence mandated constructing the second tower only after the first was leased, while keeping the Exchange operations undisturbed. Thus, the towers, although identical, had to be independently configured and engineered. The towers have separate entrances, and distinctive serrated corners create sixteen window offices per floor.

Graham, Anderson, Probst and White
20 North Wacker Drive
1927–9

Designed by Alfred Shaw (1895–1970) for Graham, Anderson, Probst, and White, the Civic Opera Building is a complex structure housing an auditorium for the Opera House, the smaller Civic Theatre, and in the middle, a 45-story office building. Samuel Insull (1859–1938), a utilities magnate, and fellow opera subscribers financed the construction of the $20 million building with the intention that office rents would support the cost of opera operations. Unfortunately, the building opened just after the 1929 stock market crash and soon both Insull and the opera were bankrupt. The Civic Opera Building is located by the river, in a former warehouse district at the western edge of the Loop, an area that was redeveloped in the 1920s. It fronts on Wacker Drive with a block-long, seventeen-bay colonnade connecting the auditorium spaces at each end; these entrances are marked by arched pediments containing sculptured bas-reliefs. Decorative details on the façade, including garlands, comedy and tragedy masks, putti, and lyres, represent music and the performing arts. Jules Guerin, also known for his watercolors of Burnham's Plan of Chicago and for the Merchandise Mart murals (see #15), was responsible for the interior design.

Kohn Pedersen Fox
2000–3

This 37-story, 700,000-square-foot office tower developed by Hines Interests is designed for large, full-floor tenants, which it quickly attracted. On a dream site facing the open corridor of the Chicago River, 191 North Wacker Drive's western façade is a tall, silver-blue glass box slab that maximizes views. This box is separated from the rear or eastern section by a notch that is 5 feet wide and 2 feet deep, and a higher roofline that contains mechanical systems enclosed in transparent glass that shows off best at night. It sits on the corner of Lake and Wacker Drive, once the site of two historic hotels: the Sauganash Hotel where Chicago's first village board election took place in 1833, and its replacement, the Wigwam Hotel, where Abraham Lincoln was nominated for president in 1860. 191 North Wacker Drive is the third office tower in a row designed by the New York architectural firm Kohn Pedersen Fox. Each one has its own look and personality. The oldest, 333 West Wacker Drive, at the bend of the Chicago River, is everyone's favorite. Next came 225 West Wacker Drive, the strong, silent type. Finally, we have 191 North Wacker Drive, a no-nonsense, corporate executive in a buttoned-down glass suit.

Kohn Pedersen Fox with Perkins & Will
1979–83

The building at 333 West Wacker Drive is a curving green glass wedge located where the Chicago River divides into its north and south branches. At this triangular site, the grid of the city meets the river bend, and the plan of this 36-story, 850,155-square-foot building is shaped by the transition between the two environments. On the Loop side, the building follows the street edges to form a truncated triangle, while above the Franklin Street entrance a notch in the glass façade creates acute angles that give a prismatic quality to the building surface. Blessed by uninterrupted view corridors, the building's river façade is a taut arc that reflects clouds, shadows, and silhouetted shapes. Internationally acclaimed and locally appreciated, sensitive to both a gentle waterway and an urban bustle, 333 West Wacker Drive is a spectacular addition to Chicago's riverfront. The three-story monumental base of polished granite and Vermont marble with a pedestrian arcade raises the office floors above the elevated train tracks at the rear of the building. Louvered medallions hide mechanical vents, becoming decorative elements in themselves and providing a visual link to the adjacent building to the east, also designed by William Pedersen.

Kohn Pedersen Fox with Perkins & Will
1985–9

This 31-story, 644,167-square-foot granite and glass skyscraper pro-vides a striking contrast to the curved green glass tower next door at 333 West Wacker Drive, which was designed by the same architect, William Pederson, a few years earlier. Known as a "contextual architect," Pedersen designs buildings that fit their urban setting by referencing exist-ing street patterns, forms, materials, and structures. For instance, 225 West Wacker Drive was the last site in the grid of the city facing the Chicago River until the river curves to form its south branch—hence the choice of masonry cladding and rectangular form typical of downtown Chicago buildings. The four spires recall the Merchandise Mart's corner towers directly across the river and are tied together by metal elements that reference the Chicago River's bridges. Although different in materi-als, shape, and size, 225 and 333 West Wacker Drive are linked by the repetition of common forms, such as the circular louvered vents, as well as by the shared horizontal street line formed by the three-story lobbies.

33 222 North LaSalle Street Building

Graham, Anderson, Probst and White
1927
Renovation and addition: Skidmore, Owings, & Merrill, 1980–6
Formerly the Builders Building

Planned as an office, distribution, and exhibition center for the construction trades and associated merchants, the Builders Building symbolizes
Chicago's building boom of the 1920s. Note the row of three-story
columns just below the cornice line of the original 1927 building that add
an element of grandeur to an otherwise foursquare mass of glazed brick
and terra cotta. In 1980, since the adjoining property was too small for a
separate building, the developer decided to add to the existing structure.
The sympathetic design of architect Adrian Smith (see #3) doubled the
size of the original building, yet matched its scale, proportions, and color;
a sloping four-story glass penthouse unifies the composition visually. The
addition's bay windows repeat the rhythm of the original building's windows but create wider views of the river and perhaps inspired those of
the hotel just across the river. As part of the restoration, marble, terra
cotta, and cast-iron pieces were carefully matched or replicated. The
LaSalle Street lobby was completely redesigned and is now a splendid
four-story-high space, complete with a skylight that had been hidden for
years.

Holabird and Root with Rebori, Wentworth, Dewey, and McCormick
221 North LaSalle Street
1929–30

Located at the head of the LaSalle Street financial district, the 41-story limestone and granite LaSalle-Wacker Building was developed by two wealthy Chicagoans, cousins Joseph Medill Patterson and Robert McCormick, for tenants associated with the banking industry. Two firms collaborated on the building; it is unclear which served as principal designer. While the building's bold, simplified setback form reflects Holabird and Root's style, most scholars attribute it to Andrew Rebori (1886–1966), based on his close associations with the McCormick family. Rebori was a talented, idiosyncratic architect whose best work exhibits an originality that challenges stylistic classification. He organized the LaSalle-Wacker Building on an H-shaped plan, with an indented central portion rising above the first 24 stories to become a wide, freestanding tower. This center setback gives the building its thronelike appearance and functions as a light well for the surrounding offices. Like several notable buildings designed during the 1920s, such as the Wrigley Building (#7) and the Tribune Tower and Printing Plant (#4), the LaSalle-Wacker Building included a lighting program—in this case a powerful rooftop beacon that showed its setbacks to an advantage.

DeStefano + Partners
Design Consultants: Taller de Arquitectura
77 West Wacker Drive
1992
Formerly known as the
R.R. Donnelley Building

Clad in white Portuguese Royal granite with a silver-gray curtain wall, this 50-story building reinterprets classical forms on a monumental scale. Decorative details are simplified; the enormous pediments that crown each façade are the building's most striking feature. Smaller gables are repeated on the doorways that punctuate the tower's 42-foot-high base. The gridded glass shaft is divided into sections by double horizontal stone bands and has notched edges that create eight corner offices per floor to take advantage of the spectacular vistas enhanced by the Chicago River's view corridor. The building lobby is designed as a museum space with sculpture and paintings by noted contemporary artists. Consulting architect Ricardo Bofill (b. 1939), who founded the Taller de Arquitectura (Architectural Workshop) in 1963 in Barcelona, Spain, is an internationally recognized modern classicist known for his inventive use of superscaled architectural elements, such as arches and columns. Other examples of his work include the Rice University School of Music in Houston, Texas, several housing projects in Spain, and the development of three new towns near Paris, France. This high-rise is his first project in Chicago.

Kevin Roche-John Dinkeloo and Associates
35 West Wacker Drive
1989

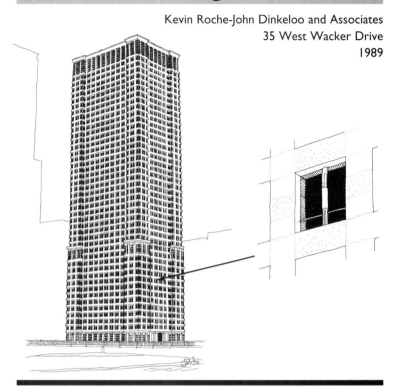

This 50-story building, with its masonry cladding, flat top, and solid shaft, projects a solid, conservative image for its major tenant, the Leo Burnett Company, Chicago's largest advertising agency. Irish-born architect Kevin Roche (b. 1922) trained at the Illinois Institute of Technology before joining Eero Saarinen's firm, which became Kevin Roche-John Dinkeloo and Associates upon Saarinen's death in 1961. The firm is well known for its corporate and museum work, and Roche himself received the prestigious Pritzker Prize in Architecture in 1982. This building, his first Chicago commission, reflects a concern for maintaining the street wall and cornice lines of existing buildings along Wacker Drive. On this highly visible site facing the Chicago River, Roche designed a skyscraper conforming to Louis Sullivan's classic definition: a clearly defined base, shaft, and capital. The building is also placed within the Chicago architectural tradition by Roche's inventive reinterpretation of the Chicago window. Here, the windows are recessed within stainless steel reveals and divided in half vertically by polished stainless steel mullions. These bars catch available light, creating a variable, sparkling surface pattern that animates the dark façade.

Jewelers Building

Thielbar and Fugard with Giaver and Dinkelberg
35 East Wacker Drive
1924–6
Later Pure Oil Building,
Now known by its address

Based on the fifteenth-century chapel for the Certosa of Pavia, an Italian monastery noted for its harmonious detail, the Jewelers Building is clad in highly decorative terra cotta tiles. Perhaps this surface ornamentation appealed to the jewelry designers, wholesalers, and retailers for whom this building was designed. Its massing, however, is simpler than its surface: a 17-story tower rises from a 24-story base and is capped with a belvedere offering panoramic views of the city to its fortunate tenant. At the twenty-fourth floor was a roof promenade and at the base of the tower was once an open-air terrace. Since the building was surrounded by public streets, adequate natural light was available without a light well, so the developers provided a parking garage in the central core, which appealed to security-conscious jewelers. Entering from lower Wacker Drive, automobiles and drivers were delivered by elevator to their parking or office floor. By 1940, mechanical problems made the garage impractical and it was converted to office space. Architects Frederick J. Thielbar (1866–1941) and John Reed Fugard (1886–1968) became partners in 1925 and designed several other buildings in Chicago. Associated architect Frederick P. Dinkelberg (c. 1869–1935) had previously worked in Daniel Burnham's office.

Harry Weese and Associates
55 East Wacker Drive
1968

In 1879, Mary Baker Eddy (1821–1910), who based her teachings on the healing methods of Jesus, organized the First Church of Christ, Scientist in Boston, Massachusetts. As the Christian Science faith flourished, additional churches were built, many of distinctive design; this Seventeenth Church of Christ, Scientist fits that tradition. Given a prominent angled site, architect Harry Weese (1915–98) used the semi-circular auditorium space to define the low, curving exterior from which rises a lead-coated, conical roof crowned with a domed lantern. The auditorium features a sound-diffusing ceiling and has 925 seats encircling the reader's platform. The church is isolated from street traffic by a lobby and has a sunken garden that admits natural light to the Sunday School one level below grade. Long horizontal windows at the base of the roof and the dome provide additional light to the auditorium. The entire façade, including the steel girders supporting the roof, is sheathed in travertine marble. Directly east is a 7-story triangular building that houses church offices, meeting rooms, mechanical systems, and other related facilities. A peaceful oasis in the middle of the city's bustle, this church is an expressive contrast to the office towers that surround it.

Mather Tower

Hubert Hugh Riddle
75 East Wacker Drive
1926–8
Renovation: Harry Weese and
Associates, 1982–3
Later Lincoln Tower,
Now known by its address

This slender, white, 42-story terra cotta tower with a lantern crown evolved from the same eclectic decorative idiom and materials as the nearby Wrigley Building, which was designed a few years earlier. Initially, owner Alonzo Mather planned twin towers (the second, at 324–30 North Michigan Avenue) that would be joined by a ground floor arcade and topped with a radio antenna. However, after the 1929 stock market crash, plans for the second tower were abandoned. Facing Wacker Drive and the Chicago River, the building is a 24-story shaft with setbacks to the rear at the ninth and sixteenth floors. The octagonal tower is set back in a series of recesses, with one tenant per floor, until the top two levels measure only 350 and 280 square feet, respectively. Designed by Herbert Hugh Riddle (1875–1939), architect of the Chicago Theological Seminary, and built at a cost of $2,617,040, Mather Tower was renovated by Harry Weese and Associates in 1983. Alonzo Mather, a descendant of New England preacher Cotton Mather, invented the Mather Stock Car for the humane transport of livestock; he is said to have been responsible for several of the building's design features, including its octagonal tower.

Alfred S. Alschuler
360 North Michigan Avenue
1922–3

As the Wrigley Building (see #7) was nearing completion, Alfred Alschuler (1876–1940) received a plum commission: the headquarters building for the London Guarantee & Accident Company, which would occupy the prominent site just across the Chicago River at the termination of Wacker Drive with the new Michigan Avenue Bridge. Alschuler was known primarily for his industrial work, although he also designed the terra cotta Thompson Building (1912) at 350 North Clark Street, the K. A. M. Isaiah-Israel Synagogue in Chicago's Kenwood neighborhood, and the old Chicago Mercantile Exchange (1927) at 110 North Franklin Street. Here, on the historic site of Fort Dearborn, he designed a 22-story Indiana limestone building using classical references throughout, from the three-story columns marking the entrance, repeated above the fifteenth floor, to the Greco-Roman tempietto on top. This aesthetic is consistent with Burnham's 1909 Plan of Chicago, which envisioned the development of the riverfront in the grand Beaux Arts tradition. Note how the rusticated base matches that of the Wacker Drive Esplanade below and how the unusual concave façade accommodates the semi-circular plaza defining the intersection of Michigan Avenue with Wacker Drive.

Holabird and Root
1927–8

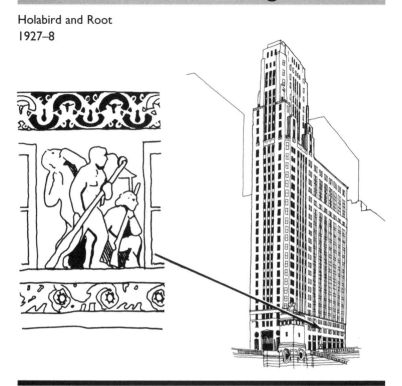

The last-built of the four original buildings located at the Michigan Avenue Bridge, 333 North Michigan Avenue resembles a slender gatepost when seen from the length of North Michigan Avenue. Clad in granite and limestone, its design reflects the sleek, Art Deco aesthetic of its time: the mass of the eleven-story tower rising from the 24-story main block is modified by a series of setbacks that emphasize its verticality, as does the absence of a cornice. At the fifth floor of the building are a series of seven-foot-high bas-reliefs by sculptor Fred M. Torrey depicting the growth and early history of Chicago: The Portage, the Hunter, Pioneer Women, the Attack on Fort Dearborn, the Covered Wagon Era, and the Traders. These reliefs harmonize with the overall massing of the building in their bold, simplified lines; they also typify the interest of the era in incorporating sculptural design into the architectural program. Holabird and Root, formed in 1928, was the successor firm to Holabird and Roche and continues to practice today. Its notable designs include the Palmolive Building (see Michigan Avenue #50), the Chicago Daily News Building (1925–9) (see #21), and the Board of Trade (1929–30) (see Loop, #8).

Office of and successor firms to Mies van der Rohe, with other firms
Bounded by East Wacker Drive, Lake Michigan, East Lake Street, and
Michigan Avenue
Begun in 1967

Illinois Center is an 83-acre development on the site of former railyards; it is planned to ultimately comprise 16 million square feet of office space, 7,500 residential units, and 3,500 hotel rooms. Since Illinois Center has a triple-decked street system east of Michigan Avenue, building entrances are high above the ground and separated from the riverfront. Pedestrian movement is primarily via an interior concourse linking buildings in the area. In the 1920s, when the land first became available for development, such notable architects as Holabird and Root and Eliel Saarinen planned dense developments. However, construction did not begin until 1967, when Mies van der Rohe designed One Illinois Center, a 30-story black glass and steel office tower. After Mies's death in 1969, his successor firm, Fujikawa, Conterato, Lohan and Associates, continued as architects, designing office towers Two and Three Illinois Center as well as Boulevard Towers. Hotel and apartment projects built more recently have added variety by using different forms and cladding materials. For example, the Swiss Grand Hotel, designed by Harry Weese and Associates, is a shiny aluminum triangle. Although pedestrian amenities have been added recently, Illinois Center would benefit greatly from more green spaces and riveredge uses.

Campus Architecture

University of Chicago

EAST 50th STREET

LAKE PARK AVENUE

8

EAST 51st STREET

55th STREET

CHICAGO R.
CHICAGO DR.

GRANT
PARK
I-290

*LAKE
MICHIGAN*

CHICAGO R.

L. SHORE DR.

Illinois
Institute of
Technology

University of
Chicago

I-90/94

WASHINGTON
PARK

MIDWAY
PLAISANCE

JACKSON
PARK

L. SHORE DR.

7

56th STREET

6

5

57th STREET

ELLIS AVENUE

SOUTH UNIVERSITY AVENUE

WOODLAWN AVENUE

LAKE SHORE DRIVE →

4

58th STREET

3

59th STREET

MIDWAY PLAISANCE

SOUTH INGLESIDE AVENUE

60th STREET

2

61th STREET

62nd STREET

63rd STREET

1 Rush University Medical Center,
Hospital Tower
2 Reva and David Logan Center for the Arts
3 University of Chicago Booth School
of Business
4 Frederick C. Robie House
5 Joe and Rika Mansueto Library
6 Max Palevsky Residential Dormitories
7 Gerald Ratner Athletic Center
8 Hyde Park Art Center
9 Crown Hall
10 State Street Village
11 McCormick Tribune Campus Center

Illinois Institute of Technology

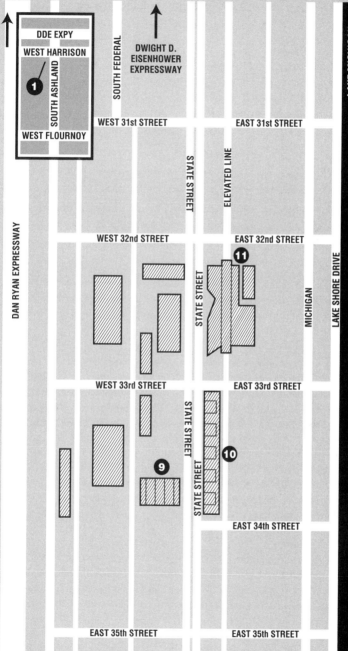

Perkins & Will
1620 West Harrison Street
2012

Hospitals are better known for services than style, but architect Ralph Johnson's new addition to the Rush University Medical Center showcases both. Most striking is the Hospital Tower's butterfly silhouette that tweaks a common hospital cruciform plan by stretching and widening the central nurse/physician station and pivoting the wings from a cross to an X. The prow-like corners, ribbon windows, and smooth metal-paneled surface recall art moderne streamlined dynamism, an appropriate model since most people see the hospital from the highway. The fourteen-story, 840,000-square-foot building is divided into three parts: a six-story rectangular base containing advanced emergency response and state-of-the-art medical intervention facilities; a recessed three-story mechanical level; and the distinctive five-story tower with 376 hospital beds. Connecting the new structure to the existing Atrium Building is the 10,000-square-foot Edward A. Brennan Entry Pavilion. Its slanted cylindrical three-story terrarium adds natural light and green elements to the lobby and is one of many features that led to the building's LEED Gold certification. Note also the green roof accessible from the fourth-floor walkway above the lobby. Rush Medical College, founded in 1837, is the oldest medical facility in Chicago; the Hospital Tower is part of an ambitious program transforming the historic West Side campus.

Tod Williams Billie Tsien Architects
915 East 60th Street
2012

The Logan Center for the Arts brings the music, theater, cinema and media studies, and visual arts departments previously scattered among several University of Chicago buildings into one distinctive complex that aims to be a "catalyst for creativity." Architects Billie Tsien (b. 1949) and Tod Williams (b. 1943), known for their spare aesthetic and cultural institution work, conceived the design as two linked forms. The first is a long, low-rise section on the south and west sides of the site that includes two theaters and a midsize performance hall, a series of art studios with a saw-toothed roof providing natural light and rooms for musical practice and university staff. Connected to it is an eleven-story glass and limestone tower that stacks floors of classrooms, areas for ensemble gatherings and spaces for the diverse creative arts. At the top is a "Performance Penthouse," with a 21-foot-high ceiling and a wall of glass offering expansive views of the university, the city, and Lake Michigan. At ground level, a courtyard links the new building to sculptor Lorado Taft's historic Midway Studios. Sitting at the southwestern edge of the campus on the far side of the Midway Plaisance, Logan Center both marks and symbolizes the University's expansion.

3　University of Chicago Booth School of Business

Rafael Viñoly Architects PC
5807 South Woodlawn Avenue
2000–4

A winter garden enclosed by soaring glazed steel arches is the heart of the new University of Chicago Graduate School of Business. On the exterior, the vaults of the arches form enormous upright funnels that are anchored by the garden structure's four columns. This bold, 5-story, 415,000-square-foot building is a dramatic example of the university's master plan to upgrade inadequate facilities and encourage a greater sense of community between students and faculty (see #6 and #7). The arches recall the gothic vocabulary of the campus and specifically reference the lancet windows of Rockefeller Chapel across the street. The building's large and complex mass is articulated in a series of setbacks designed to respect its distinguished neighbors. On the north side, the BSB steps away from the street corner to acknowledge Frank Lloyd Wright's Robie House; on the west side, it retreats more than 100 feet from its site boundary facing Rockefeller Chapel; on the south side, a grassy outdoor quadrangle acts as a transition to historic Ida Noyes Hall. Inside, spaces are layered for the three main programmatic areas: student sections are located on the main floor centered around the winter garden; administrative and faculty offices are above; and teaching facilities are below grade.

University of Chicago
Frank Lloyd Wright
5757 South Woodlawn Avenue
1908–10

The Robie House, one of Frank Lloyd Wright's (1867–1959) last Prairie School houses, is considered by many to be the culmination of his efforts to create a new architecture embodying American ideals. Frederick Carleton Robie, a young bicycle manufacturer living in the Hyde Park neighborhood in 1908, commissioned the work. Robie wanted a house filled with light that also allowed for maximum privacy. The Robie House dates from Wright's first phase as a designer of strikingly modern houses and its plan consists of parallel planes of brick, limestone, and concrete, which provide a sense of horizontality. Recessed windows combined with overhanging eaves seem to make the roof float. On the interior, space flows openly from room to room, a hallmark of Wright's planning. Walls of windows, which provide light and enclosure without cutting off views, are filled with Wright's characteristic decorative glass. No wonder the American Institute of Architects named the Robie House one of the ten most significant structures of the twentieth century. The Robie family occupied the house for only a short time; financial trouble soon forced them to sell the house. The Robie House, owned by the University of Chicago, is now operated by the Frank Lloyd Wright Preservation Trust, which is restoring the house as a museum.

5   Joe and Rika Mansueto Library

JAHN
1100 East 57th Street
2010

Helmut Jahn's design for the Joe and Rika Mansueto extension to the Regenstein Library had to solve three major problems on a small, 160- by 360-foot site: provide adequate room for collections to grow, develop attractive spaces for students to use, and improve facilities for better bibliographic preservation. His clever solution was to conceive of the building as two connected parts, one atop another. Taking a cue from major retailing warehouse systems, books are shelved far below ground in 55-foot-high racks compressed together and accessible by robotic arms controlled by computer software promising retrieval within 5 minutes. The 1,200 archival racks and 24,000 storage bins have a capacity of 3 million volumes; less than half is currently used. Aboveground is the drama: an elliptical dome rising 35 feet that is hung on a steel structure of elongated rhombuses filled with glass panels of varying transparency. At ground level, the glass is clear for viewing and natural light; as the dome rises, ceramic frits block out UV rays and solar heat. On one side of the ground floor is the Grand Reading Room for students that is fitted with furniture of light European oak; on the other, library labs for Preservation, Conservation, and Digitization.

Max Palevsky Residential Dormitories

University of Chicago
Legorreta + Legorreta
Associate Architects: VOA Associates
5630 South University Avenue, 1101 East 56th Street,
5625 South Ellis Avenue
2001–2

Mexico City-based architect Ricardo Legorreta (1931–2011), working with his son, Victor, designed this four-story, 734-bed complex of three brick buildings, each of which has a main entrance, an elevator, and a glass tower painted either purple, yellow, or pink. The residences were built along the 800 feet of 56th Street and around both corners of the block. Thus, they hold the street edge, define the corners, and form an enclosure for the Joseph Regenstein Library on the south side of the block. On the interior, doors open off the corridors into antechambers that include a private bathroom and shared space. Another set of doors then leads to two- and four-person suites, with windows facing street or courtyard. Students requested and received a lounge space for every twenty rooms, computer labs, a foreign language media center, and soundproof music practice rooms. The Legorreta team also worked with the university to modify closet space, shower heights, and electrical outlets. What is most striking about these buildings, however, is their exterior color. Although the orange-red brick matches that found in Hyde Park, the towers and details are painted in vibrant colors that contrast with the otherwise gray campus. Legorreta is known for designing places that evoke emotion through color, light, and scale.

7   Gerald Ratner Athletics Center

University of Chicago
Cesar Pelli & Associates
Associate Architects: O'Donnell, Wicklund, Pigozzi & Petersen
Architects
5530 South Ellis Avenue
2000–3

The 150,000-square-foot Gerald Ratner Athletics Center spans an entire block on South Ellis Avenue, indicating the increased demand for fitness facilities and sports programs since the university's last field house was built more than 70 years ago. It has three main sections: to the north is the Myers-McLoraine Olympic-size pool with its east-facing glass wall; to the south is the large, rectangular gymnasium. In between and recessed from the sidewalk is the entrance rotunda, the University of Chicago Hall of Fame for those students who have contributed to sports history at Chicago, and offices for the athletic faculty and staff. Cesar Pelli (b. 1926) considered the university's gothic styled buildings in an inventive way by highlighting structural expressionism. For example, in gothic architecture, flying buttresses allowed for tall, soaring spaces. Here, in a twenty-first-century interpretation, five masts, each 125 feet high—three over the pool, two over the gym—are held in place by high-strength cables and support the wave-like, 1,000-ton roof. This system makes possible the clear spans required for the gymnasium and swimming pool. Massive counterweights containing 2,500 cubic yards of concrete are buried in the ground to counteract the weight of the roof.

Garofalo Architects
5020 Cornell Avenue
2006

Often called visionary, Doug Garofalo (1958–2011) became known for exploring the role of computer technology in design both as a practicing architect and as a popular professor at the School of Architecture at the University of Illinois in Chicago. His experimental approach attracted students, colleagues, clients, and honors. The Hyde Park Art Center offers insight into his legacy: in the embrace of digital design, the collaborative approach to creative spaces, and the erasure of barriers between community and professional artist. The Center, founded in 1939 as a neighborhood arts center, led a nomadic existence until 2006 when a 32,000-square-foot Army warehouse used by the University of Chicago as a printing plant became available to the Center for $1 a year. Garofalo conceived of the building as an interactive "open canvas," gutting the interior to provide studios for visiting artists as well as including six gallery spaces, a café, a digital lab, offices, and a community resource room. Most notable is the 10- by 80-foot digital projection screen for video art integrated into the façade that becomes an ever-changing wall showing art both inside and outside. Below it, five large metal doors allow the main gallery to convert from a controlled exhibition space to an inviting public piazza.

Crown Hall

Illinois Institute of Technology
Ludwig Mies Van der Rohe
3360 South State Street
1950–6

In America, Crown Hall is both the culmination of Mies's interest in building clear span structures and the masterpiece of his campus plan for the new Illinois Institute of Technology, for which he would eventually complete twenty-two structures during his 1938–58 tenure as director of the College of Architecture. In 1950, he was asked to design a new building for the architecture and design program itself. Crown Hall's upper-level houses the College of Architecture, with an 18-foot-high ceiling and a large, column-free space created by suspending the 120- by 220-foot roof from four 120-foot-long plate girders that are each 6 feet deep. Columns on the long sides of the structure support these girders. The columns and girders are spaced to form three 60-foot bays with 20-foot cantilevers at each end. The vast room is ringed with translucent glass, above which is a section of clear glass 11 feet long. The lower level, occupied by the Institute of Design, is divided into conventional rooms lit by clerestory windows. The central entrance is reached by climbing float-ing stairs, similar to those at the elegant Farnsworth House (1946–51) in nearby Plano, Illinois, which is Mies's smaller, earlier exercise in designing a clear span steel and glass structure.

State Street Village

Illinois Institute of Technology
Murphy/Jahn
3303/3333/3353 South State Street
2001–3

State Street Village is the first new building in 30 years to be constructed on the Illinois Institute of Technology's campus. The dormitory structure both reflects and rejects the elevated train line that runs parallel and adjacent to it. The 550-foot-long curving stainless steel exterior references the silver trains that animate the site, but the building's double-pane glass and concrete muffle the sound. Five stories high, the building stretches along the east side of State Street in a series of solids and voids. It is divided into three sections that are bisected by landscaped courtyards. The corrugated stainless steel panels face the McCormick Tribune Campus Center directly north, the competition for which Jahn entered but lost in 1998. Built of poured-in-place concrete, the dormitory units are essentially raw space serviced with high-speed data connections and furnished with stainless steel furniture designed by Jahn. The first through fourth floors accommodate living for 367 students; the fifth floor is devoted to lounges and rooftop decks with views of downtown. The decks alternate with the courtyards below to create a pleasing rhythm of solid and void. Jahn himself briefly attended IIT as a Rotarian Scholar; he returned with a valuable contribution to his school.

11 McCormick Tribune Campus Center

Illinois Institute of Technology
Rem Koolhaas, Office for Metropolitan Architecture (OMA)
3201 South State Street
2000–3

Part sculpture, part gameboy, the 110,000-square-foot McCormick Tribune Campus Center is a multi-layered tour-de-force by edgy Dutch architect Rem Koolhaas (b. 1944). He first addressed the ugly adjacent elevated tracks by wrapping a 530-foot-long section in a concrete tube encased in corrugated stainless steel. Bingo! A noisy necessity transformed into industrial art. The tube's bottom becomes part of the Campus Center's ceiling. The building's programmatic requirements included a university bookstore, various offices, a post office, dining facilities, a coffeeshop/snack bar, a radio station, and a faculty club. Such prosaic campus needs are stuffed into a single-story functional playpen full of visual treats, whimsical features, interesting materials, and clever gestures. For example, to enter on State Street, one must walk through the face of Ludwig Mies van der Rohe, whose pointillist portrait is composed of familiar icons à la painter Chuck Close. Koolhaas studied the shortcuts students used to traverse the empty site, then used those pathways to differentiate required areas. Color boldly invades the subdued Miesian campus—orange for the exterior curtained walls, pale green floors and walls, and a bright red corridor of computer monitors.

Glossary

Glossary

 acroteria. A pedestal at the corners and peak of a roof to support a statue or ornament; more usually, the ornament itself.

antefix(ae). A decorated upright slab used in classical architecture to close or conceal the open end of a row of tiles that cover the joints of roof tiles.

arcade. A series of arches supported by columns or piers; a building or part of a building with a series of arches.

architrave. The ornamental moldings around the faces of the jambs and lintel of a doorway or window.

bas-reliefs. A carving, embossing, or casting moderately protruding from the background plane, from the French meaning "low-relief."

bearing wall. A wall that carries a portion of a building's weight.

belvedere. A rooftop pavilion from which a vista can be enjoyed, from the Italian meaning "beautiful view."

bifora. A double-arched opening within a larger arched frame.

brace. A metal or wood member, which may be curved (portal) or straight (knee), and is used to stiffen or support a structure.

 bundled tube. A structural system consisting of closely spaced columns tied together for strength, which, used at a building's outer wall, act as the walls of a hollow tube. The Willis Tower uses this system.

cantilever. A projecting beam or part of a structure that is supported at only one end.

cartouche. An ornamental panel in the form of a scroll, circle, or oval, often bearing an inscription.

cast iron. Smelted iron, shaped in a mold, whose compressive or load-bearing strength made it an important structural metal.

cavetto. A concave surface or molding about a quarter of a circle in section, often used in cornices, especially in Egyptian architecture.

Chicago School of architecture. High-rise commercial buildings designed in Chicago in the late nineteenth century, made possible by elevators and linked by construction similarities, including the use of a metal structural (skeleton) frame to support the building; bay, oriel, or Chicago windows to admit maximum light; and the use of the latest wind-bracing and foundation technologies.

Chicago window. A window flanked at each side by a narrow movable sash and occupying the full width of the bay in which it is placed.

coffering. A ceiling with deeply recessed, often highly ornamented panels.

console. A decorated bracket in the form of a vertical scroll, projecting from a wall to support a cornice, door, or window head.

cornice. A projecting ornamental molding along the top of a building, wall, or arch, finishing or crowning it.

crocket. In Gothic architecture, an upward-oriented ornament, often vegetal in form, regularly spaced along sloping or vertical edges of spires, pinnacles, or gables.

esplanade. A level open space for walking or driving, often providing a view.

flying buttress. A bar of masonry, usually sloping, carried on an arch, abutting a solid pier sufficient to receive the thrust of a roof or vault. A characteristic feature of Gothic construction.

footprint. The outline of a building at the ground.

light well. An open area in the center of a building used to provide natural light and ventilation, before the widespread use of electricity and air-conditioning, for the rooms or offices contained in the surrounding sides of the building.

mullion. A vertical member separating and often supporting windows, doors, or panels set in a series.

ogee. A double curve resembling an S-shape, formed by the union of a convex and a concave line.

oriel. A protruding window.

pediment. In classical architecture, the triangular gable end of a roof above the horizontal cornice; more commonly, the triangular or curved ornament used over doors or windows.

Plan of Chicago. The City of Chicago's first comprehensive planning document, prepared by Daniel Burnham and Edward Bennett, which included the development of efficient transportation systems and waterfront beautification projects. It was informed by such Beaux Arts ideas as grand boulevards, monuments, and other civic improvements.

pony truss. A low support without any overhead bracing. Structural supports are above and below the roadway.

Prairie School of architecture. A midwestern movement that sought to create buildings, chiefly residential, reflecting the flat, horizontal terrain of the Midwest and used distinctive stylized floral or geometric patterns.

quatrefoil. A four-lobed pattern divided by cusps.

rustication. Masonry cut in rough, massive blocks separated from each other by deep joints.

setback. An architectural element in which the upper stories of a tall building are stepped back from the lower stories to permit more light to reach street level.

skeleton frame. A freestanding structure of iron or steel that supports the weight of a building and on which the floors and outer covering are hung.

soffit. The underside of any architectural element.

spandrel. In a multistory building, a wall panel that fills the space between the top of a window in one story and the sill of the window in the story above.

tempietto. A small temple, especially one of ornamental character, resembling those built during the Renaissance.

terra cotta. Cast and fired clay units, usually more intricately modeled than bricks, used for decorative and/or fireproofing architectural purposes.

trunnion bascule bridge. A span that moves in a vertical plane about a horizontal axis and is supported by an axle or trunnion, a pin or pivot about which it rotates.

truss. A structure composed of a combination of members, often steel or iron, usually in some triangular arrangement so as to form a rigid framework.

Index of Architects

Please note: The names of architecture firms often change over time, and the firm name associated with a given building may vary accordingly.

A. Epstein & Sons	Associates Center	31
	Federal Center	100
	Hyatt Center	81
Abbott, Frank	Fulton House	130
Adler, Dankmar	see Adler and Sullivan	
Adler and Sullivan	The Auditorium Building	15
Alschlager, Walter W.	Medinah Athletic Club	43
Alschuler, Alfred S. (1876–1940)	London Guarantee & Accident Building	37, 151
Anderson, Peirce (1870–1924)	see Graham, Anderson, Probst and White	
Arenson, Ray	Crate & Barrel, interior	48
Atwood, Charles (1840–95)	Fisher Building	72
	Reliance Building	93
Becker, Donald N.	LaSalle Street Bridge, engineer	124
Beeby, Thomas (b. 1941)	see Hammond, Beeby and Babka; Hammond Beeby Rupert Ainge Architects	
Beman, Solon S.	Studebaker Building	16
Bennett, Edward H. (1874–1954)	LaSalle Street Bridge Houses	124
	Michigan Avenue Bridge Houses	39, 117
Bertrand Goldberg Associates	Marina City	121
	Prentice Women's Hospital and Maternity Center	135
	Raymond Hilliard Center	135
	River City	135
Bofill, Ricardo (b. 1939)	77 West Wacker Drive	146
Booth, Laurence (b. 1936)	see Booth/Hansen & Associates	
Booth/Hansen & Associates	320 North Michigan Avenue	36
	North Pier Chicago, adaptive reuse	112
	325 North Wells Street, adaptive reuse	125

Boyington, W. W.	Board of Trade	73
	Chicago Water Tower and Pumping Station	52
	Inter-State Exposition Building	20
Brownson, Jaccques (1923–2012)	Richard J. Daley Center	88
Burgee, John (b. 1933)	190 South LaSalle Street	78
Burnham, Daniel (1886–1961)	see Burnham Brothers	
Burnham, Daniel Hudson (1846–1912)	see Burnham and Root; D. H. Burnham & Co.	
Burnham, Hubert (1882–1969)	see Burnham Brothers	
Burnham and Root	Art Institute	17
	Brunswick Hotel	21
	Monadnock Building	71
	Reliance Building	93
	Rookery	76
Burnham Brothers	Bankers Building	35
	Carbide and Carbon Building	35
	Seneca Hotel	35
C. F. Murphy Associates	Federal Center	100
	First National Bank Building	97
	IBM Building	120
	Richard J. Daley Center	88
	Water Tower Place	55
	Xerox Centre	98
Cesar Pelli & Associates	Gerald Ratner Athletics Center	164
Cobb, Henry Ives (1859–1931)	Chicago Athletic Association	25
	Federal Building	100
	Palmer "castle" mansion	25
Conterato, Bruno (1925–95)	Federal Center	100
Coolidge and Hodgdon	The Art Institute of Chicago, addition	20
Cram, Ralph Adams (1862–1945)	Fourth Presbyterian Church	56

D. H. Burnham & Co.	Carson Pirie Scott and Company	94
	Conway Building	84
	First National Bank Building	97
	Fisher Building	72
	Marshall Field and Company Store	92
	Orchestra Hall	19
	Peoples Gas Company Building	21
	Railway Exchange	18
	Reliance Building	93
DeStefano, James (b. 1938)	Gateway IV	134
	see also DeStefano + Partners	
DeStefano + Partners	Sears Tower, renovation	79, 137
	77 West Wacker Drive	146
Dinkelberg, Frederick H. (c. 1869–1935)	Conway Building	84
	see also Giaver and Dinkelberg	
Drummond, William (1876–1948)	Rookery, renovation	76
Eckenhoff Saunders Architects, Inc.	Allerton House, renovation	49
Eckstorm, Christian A.	North Pier Chicago	112
Egan, James (1839–1914)	City Hall/County Building	86
Eidlitz, Cyrus W. (1858–1923)	Dearborn Street Station	104
Fellows, William K. (1870–1948)	Sears Roebuck and Company complex	103, 123
Fox, Charles (1870–1926)	see Marshall and Fox	
Frost, Charles Sumner (1856–1931)	Palmer "castle" mansion	25
Frost and Granger	Chicago and North Western Terminal	106, 133
Fugard, John Reed (1886–1968)	see Fugard and Knapp; Thielbar and Fugard	
Fugard and Knapp	Allerton House	49
Fujikawa, Conterato, Lohan and Associates	Illinois Center	153

Fujikawa Johnson and Associates	Chicago Mercantile Exchange Center	139
	Federal Center	100
Gang, Jeanne (b. 1964)	see Studio Gang Architects	
Garden, Hugh M. G. (1873–1961)	see Schmidt, Garden, and Eriksen; Schmidt, Garden and Martin	
Garofalo, Doug (1958–2011)	see Garofalo Architects	
Garofalo Architects	Hyde Park Art Center	165
Gehry, Frank (b. 1921)	see Gehry Partners, LLP	
Gehry Partners, LLP	Jay Pritzker Music Pavilion	29
Gensler	Gratz Center, Fourth Presbyterian Church	56
Giaver and Dinkelberg	Jewelers Building	148
Goettsch, James (b. 1941)	see Lohan Caprile Goettsch Architects	
Goldberg, Bertrand	see Bertrand Goldberg Associates	
Graham, Anderson, Probst and White	Civic Opera Building	140
	Continental Illinois National Bank	75
	Federal Reserve Bank	74
	Field Building	77
	Merchandise Mart	126
	222 North LaSalle Street Building	144
	Pittsfield Building	27
	Union Station	105
	Wrigley Building	40, 118
Graham, Bruce (1925–2010)	Equitable Building	41, 116
	Gateway Center	134
	Inland Steel	96
	John Hancock Center	57
	One Magnificent Mile	62
	Quaker Tower	122
	Sears Tower	79, 137
Graham, Burnham and Company	Conway Building	84
	Marshall Field and Company Store	92
Granger, Alfred Hoyt (1867–1939)	see Granger and Bollenbacher	

Granger and Bollenbacher	The Chicago Club	17
Groesbeck, Christopher (b. 1953)	Wabash Building, Roosevelt University *see* VOA Associates	14
Guerin, Jules	Civic Opera Building, interior	140
Hammond, Beeby and Babka	The Art Institute of Chicago, addition	20
	Harold Washington Library Center	66
Hammond Beeby Rupert Ainge Architects	Harris Music and Dance Theater	30
Hanna/Olin	The Art Institute of Chicago, landscape	20
Harry Weese and Associates	Campbell Courthouse Annex	70
	Fulton House, adaptive reuse	130
	Mather Tower, renovation	150
	Medinah Athletic Club, renovation	43
	River Cottages	129
	Seventeenth Church of Christ, Scientist	149
	200 South Wacker Drive	138
	Swiss Grand Hotel	153
Hasbrouck-Hunderman	Rookery, restoration	76
Hellmuth, Obata & Kassabaum	Westin Chicago River North	122
Hirsch/Bedner and Associates	Chicago Hilton and Towers, renovation	11
Holabird, John (1854–1923)	*see* Holabird and Roche	
Holabird, John Augur (1886–1945)	*see* Holabird and Root	
Holabird and Roche	Chicago Building	95
	Chicago Hilton and Towers	11
	Chicago Temple Building	85
	City and County Building	86
	Gage Group	24
	John Crerar Library	31
	Marquette Building	99
	Monadnock Building	71
	Monroe Building	22

	Old Colony Building	69
	Pontiac Building	102
	University Club	23
Holabird and Root	The Art Institute of Chicago, addition	20
	Carson Pirie Scott and Company	94
	Chicago Board of Trade	73
	Federal Reserve Bank, addition	74
	LaSalle-Wacker Building	145
	Marquette Building, renovation	99
	Michigan Square Building	55
	333 North Michigan Avenue	38, 152
	Palmolive Building	59
	Riverside Plaza	132
Holsman, Holsman, Klekamp and Taylor	860/880 North Lake Shore Drive	54
Hood, Raymond	see Hood and Howells	
Hood and Howells	Chicago Tribune Tower	42, 115
Howells, John Mead	see Hood and Howells	
Hunt, Jarvis	Chicago Tribune printing plant	115
JAHN	Joe and Rika Mansueto Library	162
	600 North Fairbanks	45
Jahn, Helmut	see JAHN; Murphy/Jahn	
Jenney, Willliam Le Baron (1832–1907)	Home Insurance Company Building	68, 77
	Leiter Building	67
	Manhattan Building	68
John Ronan Architects	Poetry Foundation	50
Johnson, Philip (1906–2005)	190 South LaSalle Street	78
Johnson, Ralph (b. 1948)	Boeing World Headquarters	131
	Rush University Medical Center, Tower Building	158
	Skybridge	107
John Vinci Associates	Carson Pirie Scott and Company, renovation	94
Kemp, Diane Legge (b. 1949)	Quaker Tower	122

Kevin Roche-John Dinkeloo and Associates	Leo Burnett Building	147
Khan, Fazlur (1928–1982)	John Hancock Center, engineer	57
	Olympia Centre, engineer	51
	One Magnificent Mile, engineer	62
	Sears Tower, engineer	79, 137
Kiley, Dan	The Art Institute of Chicago, landscape	20
Kleihues, Josef Paul (b. 1933)	Museum of Contemporary Art	53
Kohn Pedersen Fox	900 North Michigan Avenue	60
	191 North Wacker Drive	141
	311 South Wacker Drive	136
	225 West Wacker Drive	143
	333 West Wacker Drive	142
Koolhaas, Rem (b. 1944)	see Rem Koolhaas, Office for Metropolitan Architecture	
Krueck, Ron (b. 1946)	see Krueck + Sexton	
Krueck + Sexton	Spertus Institute for Jewish Learning and Leadership	13
Lagrange, Lucien (b. 1940)	see Lucien Lagrange Architects	
Legorreta, Ricardo (1931–2011)	see Legorreta + Legorreta	
Legorreta, Victor	see Legorreta + Legorreta	
Legorreta + Legorreta	Max Palevsky Residential Dormitories, University of Chicago	163
Lester B. Knight and Associates	James R. Thompson Center	87
Loebl, Schlossman and Hackl	Two Prudential Plaza	32
	Water Tower Place	55
Loebl Schlossman and Bennett	Richard J. Daley Center	88
Lohan, Dirk (b. 1938)	see Lohan Associates; Lohan Caprile Goettsch Architects	
Lohan Associates	Centennial Fountain	113
Lohan Caprile Goettsch Architects	UBS Tower	82

Lucien Lagrange Architects	Erie on the Park	128
Maher, Philip Brooks (1894–1981)	Woman's Athletic Club	47
Marshall, Benjamin (1874–1940)	see Marshall and Fox	
Marshall and Fox	Blackstone Hotel	12
	Drake Hotel	61
	Lake Shore Trust and Savings Bank	46
Martin, Edgar (1871–1951)	see Schmidt, Garden, and Martin	
McClier Corporation	Rookery, restoration	76
Mies van der Rohe, Ludwig (1886–1969)	Crown Hall, Illinois Institute of Technology	166
	Federal Center	100
	IBM Building	120
	Illinois Center	153
	860/880 North Lake Shore Drive	54
Murgatroyd and Ogden	Allerton House	49
Murphy, C. F.	Prudential Plaza, addition	32
	see also C. F. Murphy Associates; Murphy/Jahn; Naess and Murphy	
Murphy/Jahn	Chicago Board of Trade, addition	73
	James R. Thompson Center	87
	120 North LaSalle Street	83
	Ogilvie Transportation Center	106, 133
	State Street Village, Illinois Institute of Technology	167
Naess and Murphy	Federal Reserve Bank, addition	74
	Prudential Plaza	32
Netsch, Walter (1920–2008)	Inland Steel	96
Nimmons, George C. (1865–1947)	Franklin Building	103, 123
	Reid Murdoch Building	123
O'Donnell, Wicklund, Pigozzi & Petersen Architects	Gerald Ratner Athletics Center	164
Office for Metropolitan Architecture	see Rem Koolhaas, Office for Metropolitan Architecture	

Osdel, John Mills Van (1811–1891)	city offices	86
	Page Brothers Building	90
	Palmer House Hotel	90
Pace Associates	860/880 North Lake Shore Drive	54
Palmer, C. M. (1826–1902)	Palmer Building	101
Pedersen, William	see Kohn Pedersen Fox	
Pei Cobb Freed & Partners	Hyatt Center	81
Pelli, Cesar (b. 1926)	see Cesar Pelli & Associates	
Perkins and Will Partnership	First National Bank Building	97
	Standard Oil Building	33
Perkins & Will	Boeing World Headquarters	131
	Rush University Medical Center, Hospital Tower	158
	Skybridge	107
	900 North Michigan Avenue	60
	225 West Wacker Drive	143
	333 West Wacker Drive	142
Peter Lindsay Schaudt Landscape Architecture, Inc.	Hyatt Center, landscape	81
Peter Walker and Partners	UBS Tower, landscape	82
Piano, Renzo (b. 1937)	The Art Institute of Chicago, addition	20
Pihlfeldt, Thomas	LaSalle Street Bridge, engineer	124
	Michigan Avenue Bridge, engineer	39, 117
Probst, Edward (1870–1942)	see Graham, Anderson, Probst and White	
Rafael Viñoly Architects PLC	Booth School of Business, University of Chicago	160
Rapp and Rapp	Chicago Theatre	89
Rebori, Andrew (1886–1966)	Fine Arts Building Annex	14
	see also Rebori, Wentworth, Dewey and McCormick	
Rebori, Wentworth, Dewey and McCormick	LaSalle-Wacker Building	145
Rem Koolhaas, Office for Metropolitan Architecture	McCormick Tribune Campus Center, Illinois Institute of Technology	168

Riddle, Hubert Hugh (1875–1939)	Mather Tower	150
Roche, Kevin (b. 1922)	see Kevin Roche-John Dinkeloo and Associates	
Roche, Martin (1853–1927)	see Holabird and Roche	
Rochon, Pierre-Yves	Sofitel Chicago Water Tower, interior	58
Ronan, John (b. 1964)	see John Ronan Architects	
Root, John Wellborn (1850–91)	see Burnham and Root	
Root, John Wellborn, Jr. (1887–1963)	see Holabird and Root	
Schmidt, Garden, and Erikson	Federal Center	100
Schmidt, Garden, and Martin	Montgomery Ward warehouse	127
Schmidt, Richard E. (1865–1958)	Montgomery Ward & Company Building	26
	see also Schmidt, Garden, and Eriksen; Schmidt, Garden, and Martin	
Sexton, Mark (b. 1956)	see Krueck + Sexton	
Shaw, Alfred P. (1895–1970)	Civic Opera Building	140
	Field Building	77
Shaw, Howard Van Doren (1869–1926)	Cliff Dwellers Club	19
	Fourth Presbyterian Church parish house and manse	56
Shaw, Metz and Associates	The Art Institute of Chicago, addition	20
Shaw and Associates	Chicago Board of Trade, addition	73
Shepley, Rutan and Coolidge	The Art Institute of Chicago	20
	Chicago Cultural Center	28
Skidmore, Owings & Merrill	The Art Institute of Chicago, addition	20
	AT&T Corporate Center	80
	Equitable Building	41, 116
	Gateway Center	134
	Inland Steel	96
	John Hancock Center	57
	NBC Tower	114
	222 North LaSalle Street Building, renovation	144

	Olympia Centre	51
	One Magnificent Mile	62
	Quaker Tower	122
	Richard J. Daley Center	88
	Sears Tower	79, 137
	Trump International Hotel and Tower	8, 119
Smith, Adrian (b. 1944)	AT&T Corporate Center	80
	NBC Tower	114
	222 North LaSalle Street Building, renovation	144
	Olympia Centre	51
	Trump International Hotel and Tower	8, 119
Sobek, Werner	600 North Fairbanks, engineer	45
Solomon Cordwell Buenz and Associates	Chicago Hilton and Towers, renovation	11
	Crate & Barrel	48
Stone, Edward Durell (1902–1978)	Standard Oil Building	33
Studio Gang Architects	Aqua Tower	34
	Columbia College Chicago Media Production Center	10
Sullivan, Louis H. (1856–1924)	Carson Pirie Scott and Company	94
	Gage Building	24
	Stock Exchange Building	106
	Transportation Building	106
	see also Adler and Sullivan	
Summers, Gene (1923–2011)	Federal Center	100
Swanke, Hayden, Connell Architects	Chicago Board of Trade, addition	73
Taller de Arquitectura	77 West Wacker Drive	146
Thielbar, Frederick J. (1866–1941)	see Thielbar and Fugard	
Thielbar and Fugard	Jewelers Building	148
	McGraw-Hill Building	44
Tigerman, Stanley (b. 1930)	see Tigerman Fugman McCurry	

Tigerman Fugman McCurry	SelfPark	91
Tod Williams Billie Tsien Architects	Reva and David Logan Center for the Arts	159
Tomlinson, Richard	Quaker Tower	122
Tsien, Billie (b. 1949)	see Tod Williams Billie Tsien Architects	
Viguier, Jean-Paul (b. 1946)	Sofitel Chicago Water Tower	58
Vinci/Kenney	The Art Institute of Chicago, reconstruction	20
VOA Associates	Max Palevsky Residential Dormitories, University of Chicago	163
	Wabash Building, Roosevelt University	14
Waddell, John Alexander Low (1854–1938)	Loop Elevated	108
Weber, Peter J. (1864–1923)	Fisher Building, addition	72
Weese, Harry (1915–98)	see Harry Weese and Associates	
White, Howard Judson (1870–1936)	see Graham, Anderson, Probst and White	
Williams, Tod (b. 1943)	see Tod Williams Billie Tsien Architects	
Wright, Frank Lloyd (1867–1959)	Robie House	161
	Rookery, renovation	76
Yamasaki, Minoru	Montgomery Ward tower	127
Young, Hugh	Michigan Avenue Bridge, engineer	39, 117

Index of Buildings

(Italics indicate buildings referenced in text.)

A

AAllerton Crown Plaza (Allerton House), 49
Allerton House, 49
American Cold Storage Warehouse (Fulton House), 130
Aon Center, 33
Aqua Tower, 34
Art Institute, 17
Art Institute of Chicago, 20
Associates Center, 31
AT&T Corporate Center, 80
Auditorium Building, The, 15

B

Bankers Building, 35
Berghoff, The, 101
Blackstone Hotel, 12
Blackstone Theater, 12
Board of Trade, 32
Boeing World Headquarters, 131
Booth School of Business, University of Chicago, 160
Boulevard Towers, 153
Brunswick Hotel, 21
Builders Building (222 North LaSalle Street Building), 144
Burnham Center (Conway Building), 84
Butler Brothers Warehouses, 134

C

Carbide and Carbon Building, 35
Carson Pirie Scott and Company, 94
Centennial Fountain, 113
Central Office Building (Reid Murdoch Building), 123
Chase & Sanborn Coffee Warehouse (325 North Wells Street), 125
Chicago and NorthWestern Terminal, 133
Chicago and Western Indiana Railway Station (Dearborn Street Station), 104
Chicago Athletic Association, 25
Chicago Board of Trade, 73
Chicago Building, 95
Chicago Civic Center (Richard J. Daley Center), 88
Chicago Club, The, 17
Chicago Daily News Building (Riverside Plaza), 132
Chicago Hilton and Towers, 11
Chicago Mercantile Exchange, 37
Chicago Mercantile Exchange Center, 139
Chicago Public Library, 28
Chicago Public Library (Cultural Center), 28
Chicago Sun-Times Building, 119
Chicago Temple Building, 85
Chicago Theatre, 89
Chicago Theological Seminary, 150
Chicago Tribune Tower, 42, 115
Chicago Water Tower and Pumping Station, 52
City and County Building, 86
Cityfront Center, 114
City Hotel, 90
Civic Opera Building, 140
Columbia College, Media Production Center, 10
Continental Illinois National Bank, 75
Conway Building, 84

Crate & Barrel, 48
Crerar Library, 31
Crown Hall, Illinois Institute of Technology, 166

Dearborn Street Station, 104 **D**
Diana Court, 55
Drake Hotel, 61

35 East Wacker Drive **E** (Jewelers Building), 148
75 East Wacker Drive (Mather Tower), 150
Equitable Building, 41, 116
Erie on the Park, 128
Everett McKinley Dirksen Building, 100

Farwell Building, 47 **F**
Federal Center, 100
Federal Reserve Bank, 74
Field Building, 77
Fine Arts (Studebaker) Building, 16
First Methodist-Episcopal Church (Chicago Temple Building), 85
First National Bank Building, 97
First United Methodist Church (Chicago Temple Building), 85
Fisher Building, 72
Fourth Presbyterian Church, 56
Franklin Building, 103
Franklin Center (AT&T Corporate Center), 80
Frederick C. Robie House, 161
Fulton House, 130

Gage, Edson Keith, and **G** Ascher Buildings (Gage Group), 24
Gage Building, 24
Gage Group, 24
Gateway Center, 134

Gerald Ratner Athletics Center, University of Chicago, 164
Harold Washington Library **H** Center, 66
Home Insurance Company Building, 68, 77
Hotel Inter-Continental, 43
Hotel Nikko Chicago, 122
Hyatt Center, 81
Hyde Park Art Center, 165

IBM Building, 120 **I**
Ida Noyes Hall, 160
Illinois Center, 153
Illinois Institute of Technology, Crown Hall, 166
Illinois Institute of Technology, McCormick Tribune Campus Center, 167
Illinois Institute of Technology, State Street Village, 167
Illinois Merchants Bank Building (Continental Illinois National Bank), 75
Inland Steel, 96
Inter-Continental Hotel (Medinah Athletic Club), 43
Inter-State Exposition Building, 20

James R. Thompson **J** Center, 87
Jay Pritzker Music Pavilion, 29
Jewelers Building, 148
Joan W. and Irving B. Harris Music and Dance Theater, 30
Joe and Rika Mansueto Library, 162
John C. Kluczynski Office Tower, 100
John Crerar Library, 31
John Hancock Center, 57
JPMorgan Chase (First National Bank Building), 97

JPMorgan Chase (Lake Shore
Trust and Savings Bank), 46

K. A. M. Isiah-Israel   **K**
Synagogue, 37

Lake Shore Trust and   **L**
Savings Bank, 46
LaSalle Street Bridge and Bridge
Houses, 124
LaSalle-Wacker Building, 145
Lasky-Famous Player/Paramount
Studios, 10
Leiter Building, 67
Leo Burnett Building, 147
Lincoln (Mather) Tower, 150
Logan Center, 159
London Guarantee & Accident
Building, 37, 151
Loop Elevated, The, 108

Macy's (Marshall Field and   **M**
Company Store), 92
Madlener House, 127
Manhattan Building, 68
Mansueto Library, 162
Marina City, 121
Marquette Building, The, 99
Marshall Field and Company
Store, 92
Masonic Temple Building, 78
Mather Tower, 150
Max Palevsky Residential
Dormitories, University of
Chicago, 163
McCormick Tribune Campus
Center, Illinois Institute of
Technology, 167
McGraw-Hill Building, 44
Medinah Athletic Club, 43
Mercantile Exchange, 139
Merchandise Mart, 126

Metcalfe Building, 100
Metropolitan Correctional Center, 70
Michigan Avenue Bridge and
Bridge Houses, 39, 117
Michigan Square Building, 55
MidAmerica Commodity
Exchange, 134
Midway Studios, 159
Monadnock Building, 71
Monroe Building, 22
Montgomery Ward & Company
Building, 26
Montgomery Ward warehouse
complex, 127
Morton International
Building (Boeing World
Headquarters), 131
Museum of Contemporary Art, 53

NBC Tower, 114   **N**
North Fairbanks, 45
860/880 North Lake Shore
Drive, 54
120 North LaSalle Street, 83
222 North LaSalle Street
Building, 144
320 North Michigan Avenue, 36
333 North Michigan Avenue, 38,
152
900 North Michigan Avenue, 60
919 North Michigan Avenue
(Palmolive Building), 59
North Pier Chicago, 112
191 North Wacker Drive, 141
325 North Wells Street, 125
Northwestern Atrium (Ogilvie
Transportation Center), 106, 133

Ogilvie Transportation   **O**
Center, 106, 133
Old Colony Building, 69

Olympia Centre, 51
One Magnificent Mile, 62
One Prudential Plaza, 32
Orchestra Hall, 19
Oriental Theatre, 89

Page Brothers Building, 90   **P**
Palmer Building. See Stone
  and Palmer Buildings (The
  Berghoff)
Palmer House Hotel, 90
Palmolive Building, 59
Peoples Gas Company Building, 21
Pittsfield Building, 27
Plaza Escada, 128
Poetry Foundation, 50
Pontiac Building, 102
Prentice Women's Hospital and
  Maternity Center, 135
Prudential Plaza, 32
Pugh Warehouse (North Pier
  Chicago), 112
Pure Oil Building (Jewelers
  Building), 148

Quaker Tower, 122   **Q**
Quincy Park, 138

R. R. Donnelly Building, 146   **R**
Railway Exchange, 18
Raymond Hilliard Center, 135
Regenstein Library, 162
Reid, Murdoch and Company, 103
Reid Murdoch Building, 123
Reliance Building, 93
Reva and David Logan Center for
  the Arts, 159
Richard J. Daley Center, 88
River City, 135
River Cottages, 129
Riverfront Park, 122
Riverside Plaza, 132

Robie House, 161
Rockefeller Chapel, 160
Rookery, 76
Roosevelt University Auditorium
  Building, 14
Rush University Medical Center,
  Hospital Tower, 158

Santa Fe Building, 18   **S**
Sauganash Hotel, 141
Schlesinger and Mayer Store
  (Carson Pirie Scott and
  Company), 94
Sears Roebuck and Company, 103,
  123
Sears Tower, 79, 137
Second Leiter Building, 67
SelfPark, 91
Seneca Hotel, 35
Seventeenth Church of Christ,
  Scientist, 149
Skybridge, 107
Sofitel Chicago Water Tower,
  58
190 South LaSalle Street, 78
224 South Michigan Avenue
  (Railway Exchange), 18
200 South Wacker Drive, 138
311 South Wacker Drive, 136
Spertus Institute for Jewish
  Learning and Leadership, 13
Standard Oil Building (Aon
  Center), 33
State of Illinois Center (James R.
  Thompson Center), 87
State Street Village, Illinois
  Institute of Technology, 167
Stevens Hotel. see Chicago
  Hilton and Towers
Stock Exchange Building, 106,
  133

Stone and Palmer Buildings (The Berghoff), 101
Studebaker Building, 16
Sullivan Center (Carson Pirie Scott and Company), 94
Swiss Grand Hotel, 153
Symphony Center (Orchestra Hall), 19

Thompson Building, 37 **T**
Tivoli Theatre, 89
Transportation Building, 106, 133
Trump International Hotel and Tower 8, 119
Two Prudential Plaza, 32

UBS Tower, 82 **U**
Union Station, 105
University Club, 23
University of Chicago, Booth School of Business, 160
University of Chicago, Gerald Ratner Athletics Center, 164
University of Chicago, Max Palevsky Residential Dormitories, 163

University of Chicago, Robie House, 161
Uptown Theatre, 89

Wabash Building, Roosevelt **W**
University Academic and Student Life Center, 14
Water Tower. see Chicago Water Tower and Pumping Station
Water Tower Place, 55
Westin Chicago River North (Riverfront Park), 122
55 West Monroe (Xerox Centre), 98
77 West Wacker Drive, 146
225 West Wacker Drive, 143
333 West Wacker Drive, 142
Wigwam Hotel, 141
William J. Campbell U.S. Courthouse Annex, 70
Willis (Sears) Tower, 79, 137
Woman's Athletic Club, 47
Wrigley Building, 40, 118

Xerox Centre, 98 **X**